Imagined Cities

Imagined Cities

Urban Experience and the Language of the Novel

ROBERT ALTER

Yale University Press New Haven & London

Published with assistance from the foundation established in memory of Philip Hamilton McMillan of the Class of 1894, Yale College.

Designed by James J. Johnson and set in Monotype Bell type by Binghamton Valley Composition.
Printed in the United States of America by Sheridan Books.

Library of Congress Cataloging-in-Publication Data
Alter, Robert.
Imagined cities : urban experience and the language of the novel / Robert Alter.
p. cm.
Includes bibliographical references and index.
ISBN 0-300-10802-8 (cloth : alk. paper)
1. European fiction—19th century—History and criticism.   2. European fiction—20th century—History and criticism.   3. Cities and towns in literature.   I. Title.
PN3352.C5A48 2005
809.3'9321732—dc22   2004026801
A catalogue record for this book is available from the British Library.

10   9   8   7   6   5   4   3   2   1

For Steve and Hannah Aschheim
with affection

Contents

Preface

The intimate relationship between the novel and the city is likely to stare most readers in the face, and it has understandably been the subject of voluminous, and at times tedious, critical discussion. If the audience and the concerns of the novel have been predominantly bourgeois, and if the novel, the only major genre to emerge after the invention of the printing press, is the modern literary genre par excellence, it makes perfect sense that novels should repeatedly focus on the city, the principal theater of bourgeois life and also the form of collective existence that undergoes the most spectacular, dynamic growth throughout the modern period.

Most considerations of this large topic, however, have concentrated in one way or another on how the material realities of the city are registered in the novel. This concentration is equally evident in old-fashioned critics who naïvely or at least unreflectively embrace the notion of literary realism and in recent critics, whether latter-day followers of Marx or of Foucault or of both. Critics, that is, of both the old dispensation and the new are predisposed to speak about how the novel "represents" or "reflects" the reality of the city. What, they ask, can one learn from reading the novels of the era about the slums of London, the sewers of Paris, the new shopping arcades of the nineteenth-century metropolises; about such institutions as the stock market, prostitution, fashion, and the theater; about class relations, social mobility, the mechanisms of power, and the new economic pressures of urban life?

Such questions, of course, are not irrelevant to the kinds of aims that many novelists, especially in the nineteenth century, actually had in mind, with some of the writers imagining their activity as a kind of uniquely privileged form of reportage about the contemporary world. But there is a qualitative difference between journalism and fiction writing that the focus on the representation of material reality and social institutions tends to blur, and there may be inherent limits on the access of the novelistic imagination to objective, collective realities. To write a novel, after all, is to re-create the world from a highly colored point of view—inevitably, that of the novelist, and, often, that of the principal character as well. This strong mediation of an individual imagination is as clearly manifested in a novelist such as Emile Zola who claims to be a scrupulously empirical student of contemporary society as it is in a lyric novelist such as Virginia Woolf.

One decisive development in the novel through the late decades of the nineteenth century and on into the twentieth (the time span under view in the chapters that follow) is the practice of conducting the narrative more and more through the moment-by-moment experience—sensory, visceral, and mental—of the main character or characters. This general procedure, which I shall call experiential realism, can be central to the narrative even when the novelist is also minutely concerned with social and material realia. It is the intersection of the subtle deployment of experiential realism and the emergence of a new order of urban reality that is the subject of the considerations offered here of a line of novelists from Flaubert to Kafka and Joyce. The great European cities grew exponentially from the beginning of the nineteenth century to the early decades of the twentieth. (American cities also grew rapidly during this period but were much less subjected to novelistic attention, and it was a development that took place in a cultural context so different from Europe's that it seems prudent not to attempt discussing both in a single framework here.) There is abundant evidence, much of it extraliterary, that this runaway growth of the city effected certain fundamental transformations in the nature of urban experience. Whatever the new objective realities, from architecture to public transportation to the economy, it felt different for individuals to live in this new urban zone—to walk the city streets, to enter into the urban crowds, to be exposed to the exponential increase of noise and bustle, to inhabit an apartment building or a tenement in the new demographic density of the city. The perception of the fundamental categories of time and space, the boundaries of the self, and the autonomy of the individual began to change. What novelists managed to be progressively more subtle and more persuasive in registering, what sets them off from journalists, is the shifting pulse of experience felt by the individual, how the mind and the senses take in the world, construct it, or on occasion are confounded by it.

The experiential realism of the novel as a searching response to the felt new reality of the European city leads me to begin with Flaubert and not with Balzac, who otherwise might seem a more obvious point of departure. It equally takes the story I am trying to tell all the way to Kafka, who might at first appear to have no bearing whatever on the novelistic rendering of any real historical city but who proves to be an instructive instance of the novel's function as a seismograph of modern urban experience. In regard to literary history, this investigation begins in the late nineteenth century at a moment when one can detect, at least retrospectively, forerunners of modernism. It ends with four novels that appeared in the 1920s, at the zenith of what is now often called High Modernism. That stopping point is by no means intended to imply that little of interest in the novel-

istic treatment of the city has occurred since, but the 1920s do
mark the completion of a certain arc of development that began
in prose fiction with Flaubert (and perhaps in poetry with
Baudelaire). On the historical plane, major cities in the developed world have continued to grow over the past eight decades,
but at a slower rate than before, and they seem well beyond the
terrific disorientation of transition triggered by the mushrooming of urban centers from the beginning of the nineteenth century to the first three decades of the twentieth. In any case, my
choice of novels is plainly meant to be suggestive rather than
comprehensive. These discussions are intended not as a grand
narrative about the history of the novel and the modern city
(by now, one is entitled to be skeptical about most grand narratives) but rather as a selective sampling that highlights one
central line of development in what remains a variegated picture.
I would hope that this investigation has more than antiquarian
interest because I think that the line of development reflected
in these books may still have urgent things to say to us as
dwellers of cities in which, along with the excitements of urban
life, problems proliferate much faster than solutions.

The two chapters on Flaubert were first presented at New York
University in the fall of 2002 as the Remarque Lectures in European Culture. I am grateful to Tony Judt, the director of the
Remarque Institute, for inviting me to give the lectures and also
for arranging a faculty seminar on the subject of the lectures
that provided valuable intellectual stimulation. The two Flaubert lectures, followed by an additional six, then became the
Weidenfeld Lectures in European Comparative Literature that I
gave at the University of Oxford in the spring of 2003. I would
like to thank in particular Tony Nuttall, of the Weidenfeld
Committee, for inviting me to present the lectures, and Dame
Ruth Deech, principal of St. Anne's College, for her hospitality.
The manuscript was read by my dear friends Michael Bernstein

and Tom Rosenmeyer, and I am grateful for their astute comments.

Secretarial and research expenses for this book were covered by funds from the Class of 1937 Chair in Comparative Literature at the University of California at Berkeley. My thanks to Janet Livingstone for her faithful work in typing the manuscript.

Imagined Cities

1

Flaubert

The Demise of the Spectator

O<small>F ALL THE TERMS INVOKED</small> to register what the novel does with reality—represent it, reflect it, distort it, invent it, evade it, depending on the critic's approach—the most indispensable and also the most slippery is *language*. We know well enough what is meant when we say that French and Italian are different languages, but it is not self-evident whether "the language of fiction" is more than a loose metaphorical application of the term to literature. The role of language for the twentieth-century theorist who has most powerfully shown its centrality to our cultural experience, M. M. Bakhtin, is symptomatic of the prevailing terminological confusion. Very occasionally, when Bakhtin says "language" he actually means something unambiguous like Russian or French. Far more often, he uses the term to indicate what a linguist would call a sociolect—the particular version of an approximately shared language that reflects the values, interests, and ideology of one class, subgroup, or political or even vocational solidarity within the general society. This fluidity of usage is compounded by Bakhtin's tendency to employ *word*, *voice*, and *language* as rough equivalents, and he is not alone in such looseness.

In some rudimentary sense, the everyday discourse of a culture, whether spoken or written, and its fiction obviously manifest the same language, and some novelists have taken pains to
stress the sameness, as famously illustrated by Stendhal's declaration that his novels were written in the style of the civil
code. No one would dispute that *The Charterhouse of Parma* and
the government directives of the July Monarchy are equally
written in French, and Louis Philippe's functionaries would have
needed no special dictionary to decipher the novels of Stendhal.
This obvious continuity between the language of literature and
language in its ordinary usage must be granted, and yet there
is a whole set of distinctive practices in the novelistic deployment of language that become increasingly refined in the course
of the nineteenth century in an effort, I shall argue, to make the
novel a more adequate vehicle for representing what is largely
perceived as a new kind of reality. These technical refinements,
in turn, will be assimilated and boldly extended by the modernists during the first quarter of the twentieth century.

The disjunction between the language of fiction and the language of quotidian communication has been rigorously defined
in technical linguistic terms by Ann Banfield in her memorably
titled study *Unspeakable Sentences.*[1] She painstakingly demonstrates that there are sentence-types that can occur only in narrative fiction, not in ordinary discourse, that narrative fiction
adapts the tense system of the general language in a specialized
way to constitute a wholly different order of temporality, which
also involves a set of deictics, or "pointing words," that function
quite differently from the way they would in extrafictional usage. Her analysis leads to the conclusion that the language of
fiction develops its own grammar and syntax, in certain respects
only superficially resembling the grammar and syntax of ordinary discourse, and that it lacks the practical communicative
function of extraliterary language. As a Chomskian linguist,
Banfield believes that the distinctive features of language which
she describes emerge more or less spontaneously as a universal

property of language generated by the differing potentials of speech and writing. My own focus will be on elements of the watershed experience of nineteenth-century European history that may have driven this collective experiment in the reshaping of language in the novel. I shall make no pretense to technical linguistic analysis, and because most of the great novelists are, after all, people with an acute and original aesthetic sense manifesting itself in the medium of words, I shall be especially concerned with how the language of the novel is embodied in the *style* of particular novels.

The introduction of new technologies, and the new arrangements of public and private space and of social relations with which these technologies interacted and which they to some degree engendered, changed the ways Europeans experienced the fundamental categories of time and space, as Wolfgang Schivelbusch has shown in illuminating detail in his study of the effects of the railroad on nineteenth-century imaginations. Let me cite one exemplary instance that he considers, the effect of the radically new glass architecture used for the railway terminals, which imposed on processes of perception a general impression he sums up in the word *evanescence:*

> The uniform quality of the light and the absence of light-shadow contrasts disoriented perceptual faculties used to those contrasts, just as the railroad's increased speed disoriented the traditional perception of space. The motion of the railway, proceeding uniformly and in a straight line, was experienced as abstract, *pure* motion, dissociated from the space in which it occurred. Analogously, the space of ferro-vitreous architecture appeared as pure and abstract light-space, dissociated from all customary architectural form, a space without qualities and contrasts.[2]

I would like to propose a second step in this sort of analysis by addressing the means through which literature (like painting, photography, and then film) fashions an innovative language to represent this basic shift in modern consciousness. The great locus of historical dynamism in the nineteenth century—both an engine of change and its consequence—was the city. Throughout Europe, there were waves of migration from the provinces to the cities (Paris, London, Petersburg, Vienna), especially on the part of young males seeking new economic and social opportunities. There is evidence that toward the bottom of the social ladder, large numbers of young women as well migrated to the cities, chiefly peasant girls seeking urban jobs as servants. With few exceptions, however, this group remained below the threshold of novelistic representation, which for the most part concentrated on the middle classes. Here the migrants were typically young men, and the demographic movement they constituted was mirrored in a recurrent novelistic plot that Lionel Trilling aptly called the story of the Young Man from the Provinces—one thinks of Balzac's Rastignac and Lucien de Rubempré, Stendhal's Julien Sorel, Dickens's Pip, Dostoevsky's Raskolnikov. Novelists of the period were, of course, also often interested in what George Eliot announced in her subtitle for *Middlemarch* as "A Study of Provincial Life," but it is the new nineteenth-century city that was the most compelling theater for the playing out of the realist enterprise in the novel.

No setting provided a more powerful stimulus for this enterprise than Paris. In a famous poem, "Le Cygne" (The swan), Baudelaire saw the streets of Paris as the very embodiment of wrenching historical change. In the first half of the nineteenth century, the population of the city doubled. By 1860, a scant few years after Baudelaire's poetic reflection on the disappearance of the remembered city, Paris had incorporated the surrounding suburbs into the municipality, thus increasing its population by another third and doubling the area of the city. To this demographic and geographic expansion one must add the constant pressure of explosive political change. As many commentators have observed, what above all makes Paris the crucible for historical transformation in nineteenth-century Europe is that it is the principal European arena of revolution—in 1789, in 1830, in 1848, and in 1871, with a more or less chronic anxiety at least in some circles about potential upheaval in between those dates.

The overall effect of this mushrooming new urban reality was, as the novels of the period vividly attest, exciting, intoxicating, bewildering, and scary. A youthful immigrant from the provinces trying to make his way in Paris might have a shifting circle of friends but hardly a stable community. (People from the provinces also sometimes moved to the metropolis in family units, but as with the peasant class, groups of this sort were rarely the object of representation in the novel, given its generic commitment to tracing the fate of individuals.) The opportunities of social and economic upward mobility might ignite the new urbanite's imagination, but the competitive ruthlessness of the metropolis could easily daunt and defeat him, and his own daily condition was likely to be the state of deracinated isolation for which the Sorbonne sociologist Emile Durkheim would later coin a name—*anomie*. The metaphors for Paris characteristically elaborated by the novelists are a vast harem (sexual as well as economic opportunity beckons in it), a brilliant emporium (or alternately, a brawling marketplace), an exotic human and architectural wonderland, a battlefield, an inferno.

But beyond such no doubt extravagant metaphorical gestures, how was a writer to cope with this new reality in the language of fiction? The decisive figure in this story as I see it is not Balzac—who is in fact the preeminent purveyor of most of the metaphors for the city just cited—but Flaubert. His one great Parisian novel, *The Sentimental Education* (1869), extends the technical innovations of *Madame Bovary*, but as narrative and as a vision of human value in the context of nineteenth-century history, it is more radical than its predecessor, and in particular its representation of the city anticipates the great modernists who read Flaubert with keen attention.

Before we look into Flaubert, I should like to register a

conviction of critical methodology. Many recent discussions of the novel, whether inflected by the New Historicism, specifically by Foucault, or by Marxism, or by feminism, stress the key role of historical contexts in determining what is sometimes referred to in marxisant language as "literary production." We of course need to know about contexts, and no sane critic will imagine that the achievements of literature miraculously spring out of a vacuum. What I shall resist in my own procedure is the notion that literature is fundamentally a reflex of ideology; or that it is primarily a manifestation of formal potentials inherent in language, as Ann Banfield seems to suggest; or that it is to be understood in collective terms as an evolution of literary codes, as Margaret Cohen has argued in her sedulously researched, though in some respects not altogether convincing, *The Sentimental Education of the Novel*.[3] To concentrate on the peak achievements of individual writers is sometimes referred to pejoratively as a "monumentalizing" of literary history. Granted, it enlarges our sense of what literature is about to have some overview of the whole literary marketplace such as Cohen provides in considering nineteenth-century sentimental fiction written by women, but one hardly needs reference to, let us say, Barbara Cartland, author of several hundred vastly popular and completely formulaic romances, in order to see that Margaret Atwood at her best is a fresh and original novelist working in a wholly different order of imaginative art. I suppose that by this late moment in the era of suspicion, *genius* may be an altogether taboo term for critical discourse, but some equivalent of it seems necessary to describe the breakthrough Flaubert effected in perfecting a technique, *le style indirect libre* (following Dorrit Cohn, I shall call it narrated monologue), that had been intermittently deployed by others—in the early nineteenth century, sometimes by Jane Austen and Stendhal. Allied with other equally important techniques for representing a character's point of view, narrated monologue in Flaubert became the instrument for expressing a new sense of reality.

Why does this story begin with Flaubert rather than with Balzac? Balzac patently set himself the task of becoming the bard of the new metropolis, and the standard surveys of "the city in literature" quite properly devote considerable attention to him. But Balzac represents the city from a standpoint of assumed authority that does not do full justice to the kinetic and disorienting reality of the new nineteenth-century urban scene. To begin with, for all his attention to the observable details of the Parisian cityscape, from the new shopping arcades to the run-down *quartiers* that harbored crime and prostitution, Balzac is more a mythographer of Paris than a realist witness to the experience of the city. He loves to invoke the imagery of traditional mythology in order to suggest the grandeur, the intensity, the conjunction of extremes that he sees in Paris. The terms in which he represents the city are insistently hyperbolic and reflect a fondness for extravagant and symmetrical antitheses. Balzac self-consciously "does" Paris in a series of rhetorical set pieces of varying length scattered through his novels. An exemplary instance is the long introductory section of *The Girl with the Golden Eyes*, in which he conjures up for the reader a kind of three-sided apartment building that allows him to exhibit the tenants transparently in ascending social order, from the proletarians on the ground floor to the petty bourgeois above them and upward through the legal professions and the artists to the aristocrats on top. As mythographer of Paris, he invites us to see it through one metaphorical lens after another—sinister masquerade, steamship, battlefield, and, above all, inferno. This fondness for metaphor, always linked with an eagerness to proclaim moral meanings, leads to an allegorization of the city. Here is a characteristic passage (which I offer in Carol Cosman's recent, wonderfully apt English version):

> The city, then, can have no greater morality, friendly feeling, or cleanliness than the boiler engines of those magnificent steamships that you admire as they cut through the waves! Paris is

indeed a superb vessel laden with intelligence. Yes, her coat of arms is one of the oracles sometimes allowed by fate. The CITY OF PARIS has her tall bronze mast engraved with victories and with Napoleon at the helm. This craft may pitch and roll, but she plows through the world of men, fires through the hundred mouths of her tribunes, furrows the seas of science full steam ahead, cries through the voices of her scholars and artists: "Forward, march! Follow me!"[4]

At moments such as this, one feels that Balzac's literary myth of Paris is less a representation of the city than impassioned promotional material for it. What matters above all is the idea that Paris, whatever its outrageous contradictions and its hellish faces (or rather *because* of them), is the place where things happen, the place to which all the world turns. The odd insertion here of Napoleon and the motif of victories a decade and a half after the debacle of Waterloo is an instructive symptom of this impulse to set Paris at the vanguard of history, even in defiance of its actual political fortunes.

Peculiarly intertwined with the project of creating a literary myth to persuade us of the portentous importance of the city is the sustained effort of the Balzacian narrator to serve as authoritative guide to Paris. Actual guidebooks to Paris began to appear in the late eighteenth century and proliferated through the nineteenth, as Priscilla Parkhurst Ferguson has shown in instructive detail.[5] Balzac appears to have appropriated the instructional purposes of the guidebook for the world of his novels, reinforcing them with the terms of reference of taxonomical science (most famously, zoology). What I would stress is that, though he is one of the master storytellers of European literature, the language of his Parisian-guide passages is not the language of narrative fiction. It is precisely in these passages that Gérard Genette's famous distinction between *récit* and *discours* in Balzac is decisively important. Balzac in the passages when he is playing the role of Parisian guide does not deploy a distinctive language of fiction to body forth a story of unfolding

experience in the city. Instead, his language is expository, de-
clarative, abounding in rhetorical balance and antithesis, revel-
ing in inventory-like catalogues, insisting on thematic unities.
("Gold and pleasure," we are told repeatedly in the overture to
The Girl with the Golden Eyes, are the keys to everything that
happens in Paris.) He presents himself as a practitioner of "the
science of manners," and because he is French, this means that
his pronouncements often come in weighty aphorisms: "In Paris,
vanity is the sum of all passions"; "Pleasure is like certain me-
dicinal substances: To maintain the same effects you must double
the dose, and this inevitably leads to death or brutishness." Authoritative declarations on the nature of the animal and habitat
under consideration are flourished as certainties: "The Parisian
is interested in everything and, in the end, interested in nothing.
. . . The Parisian, regardless of age, lives like a child. . . . In Paris,
no emotion can resist the drift of things, and the struggle to
swim against the tide dampens the passions" (pp. 2, 3).

As a rhetorical performance, all this is executed with great
brilliance and energy, and from our late-modern point of view,
it has an abiding charm. Few major writers after 1850 will follow this Balzacian path because few are willing to pretend to
the magisterial certitude that informs his discursive accounts of
the city. To many, the metropolis will seem increasingly a theater of perplexity, defying summation, lacking social, political,
and therefore thematic coherence. It was Flaubert who would
fashion a language to register this sense of the city.

I have so far not invoked the figure of the *flâneur* that, most
probably through the pervasive influence of Walter Benjamin,
has become for many indispensable in any consideration of literary responses to nineteenth-century Paris. The flâneur is the
idling pedestrian, the curious, perhaps disinterested, purposeless
observer of teeming urban variety, the spectator connoisseur. At
the beginning of the second chapter of his short novel *Ferragus,*
Balzac offers a grand catalogue of flâneurs, whom he calls by
that name or simply designates "pedestrians" or even "foot-

soldiers of Paris." Paris is conceived as a place of scintillating
energies, exemplified here by the grand display of running water
bursting from drain spouts and rolling across rooftops in a rain-
storm. All this and "finally a thousand other remarkable noth-
ings [are] studied with delight by the flâneurs." The position
of Balzac's narrator, then, which is virtually explicit here and
implicit throughout his fiction, is of a super-flâneur, compre-
hending all the individual flâneurs in his commanding overview
while sharing with them the piquant, untiring curiosity of spectatorship, which at moments comes to seem virtually the rationale for his telling the story of these Parisian lives riven by
passions and jealousies and terrible obsessions.

The story of futility and frustration that constitutes the repeatedly short-circuited plot of *The Sentimental Education* registers the decline of the flâneur, the death of spectatorship. At
first blush, this may sound like a surprising claim because the
protagonist, Frédéric Moreau, as a character ultimately capable
of doing nothing, would appear to be someone who in fact constantly substitutes spectatorship for living. Flaubert's shrewder
perception is that the individual, caught in the shower of exciting and conflicting stimuli of the urban milieu, can see them
only through the distorting medium of his private preoccupations (for which Flaubert invents a narrative technique), and
that the flâneur as disinterested spectator is chiefly a literary
fiction. It is instructive that the one moment in the novel when
Frédéric becomes a genuine flâneur is the very moment that
ought to make mere spectatorship an outrageous contradiction—
the violence of the revolution of 1848. Here is Frédéric, just
having returned from an idyllic interlude in the country with
his newly acquired mistress Rosanette, walking through the
zone of combat:

> The drummers sounded the attack. Sharp cries, triumphant
> cheers, were raised. A constant surge shook the crowd. Fré-
> déric, caught between two dense masses, did not budge, fasci-

nated in any case and enjoying himself immensely. The wounded who were falling, the dead sprawled out, did not have the look of real wounded, of real dead. It seemed to him that he was attending a performance.[6]

The stance of the flâneur as amused observer in these circumstances of life and death is, of course, a serious problem and perhaps even the symptom of a pathology. Frédéric's disengaged spectatorship has the effect of draining the world around him of reality, reducing lethal conflict to make-believe performance (*spectacle*). What in this instance makes this peculiar stance possible for him is precisely the sheer extremeness of the events he is witnessing. The drumrolls and the rifle shots and the falling bodies are sufficiently startling that for once he can forget his romantic obsession with Mme Arnoux and his erotic entanglement with Rosanette and his vague but compelling dreams of glory and give himself over to the pleasures of observation. What he is manifestly incapable of doing, in perfect consistency with his general penchant for floating with the surface tide of experience rather than immersing himself in it (how fitting that the novel begins with Frédéric on a steamboat headed up the Seine), is entering into the scene he observes, actually engaging its political or moral reality. His moment as pure flâneur is an exposure of the emptiness of spectatorship.

Let us compare this scene of Frédéric observing revolution as sheer theater with an earlier scene in the novel that might seem to be a classic instance of the protagonist as flâneur but in fact proves to be something rather different. The passage is too long to quote in full, but I shall try to offer a strategic summary. Frédéric, by this time a frequent though frustrated visitor to the Arnoux apartment, is, as usual, mooning over Mme Arnoux: "As he had no work, his lack of occupation reinforced his melancholy." He spends hours on his balcony, looking down at the quays of the Seine, the Notre Dame bridge, the Hôtel de Ville, the dome of the Tuileries. Restless, he goes back inside his room, stretches out on his couch to surrender to a stream of fitful reflections, then goes out to roam the streets, where his observation of shops and craftsmen and wagons and buildings and other pedestrians has a superficial kinship with the activity of a Balzacian flâneur. But making his way through the noise and dust and bustle of the city streets, he is neither curious about what he encounters nor, as in the battle scene, entertained by it: "He felt himself entirely disgusted by the crudeness of the faces, the silliness of the remarks, the stupid satisfaction secreted in sweat on the foreheads. And yet, the awareness of being worth more than these men mitigated the fatigue of looking at them" (p. 117). Fatigue would be the farthest thing from the mind of the true flâneur looking with curiosity at people and places in the urban setting. Frédéric, on the other hand, is exhausted and disgusted by looking at the street scene because the crude and anonymous urban crowd confronts him with his own nullity—to which he responds defensively with a characteristic fantasy of superiority, unwarranted by anything he has actually ever done.

Behind the observed surfaces, moreover, of the Parisian panorama flickers a purely projected image that is the real object of Frédéric's attention. As he looks from his balcony at one end of his field of vision to the dome of the Tuileries defined against the horizon, he thinks, "It was behind there, in that direction, that Mme Arnoux's place must be." The verb of supposition, "must be," *devait être*, is the linguistic indicator of narrated monologue, in this case the clue to a mind not so much taking in the world as straining to see through it the lineaments of its own obsession. Toward the end of this long passage, as Frédéric continues to pace the streets, every woman he meets, every piece of merchandise displayed that catches his eye, carries his imagination back to the absent woman of his desires, with this apt summary of his monomania: "Paris referred to her presence, and the great city hummed, like a vast orchestra, around her" (p. 120).

Technically, *The Sentimental Education* is remarkable for the meticulous precision with which everything is rendered from the point of view of the protagonist. This represents, of course, a set of narrative techniques that Flaubert had perfected fifteen years earlier in *Madame Bovary*, but whereas in his novel of provincial life they chiefly realize the agitated and fantasy-ridden inner world of the protagonist, here they serve simultaneously to convey Frédéric's inner world—like Emma, he is an addict of fantasy—and the distinctive character of the urban environment that impinges on him. I do not mean in any way to diminish the importance in literary history or the formal brilliance of the technical innovations of *Madame Bovary*. Provincial life, as I have already noted, remained a repeated focus of the nineteenth-century novel, and this particular novel of provincial life, with all its technical finesse, was no doubt far more widely read than *The Sentimental Education*. Narration through the point of view of the principal character works beautifully to convey Emma's isolation in a relentlessly banal provincial town as well as her entrapment in romantic and erotic fantasies nourished by reading. But when Flaubert turned this same set of narrative techniques on the urban realm, they became the means of representing a kind of complicity between the consciousness of the protagonist and the nature of the city itself and thus took on a new role in registering a historical transition. Sometimes the internalization of narrative involves an intimation of his unspoken inner language (which is to say, narrated monologue, an interior monologue mediated by the narrator). Often, the focus is on his visual or even auditory perspective. Here is a small and characteristically elegant instance, in this case involving the shared vantage point of Frédéric and Rosanette as they return to the city at night in a rented two-wheel carriage from an outing to the Bois de Boulogne: "Finally, they returned through the Arc de Triomphe and the great avenue, breathing in the air, with the stars over their heads, and, to the very end of the perspective, all the gas lights linked up in a double row of lu-

minous pearls" (p. 429). The metaphor drawn from the semantic
field of precious ornaments signals the marked aestheticizing
tendency in Flaubert's rendering of the cityscape, though the
aesthetic finish and even the particular association with jewels
are in this instance motivated by the mood of lovers' euphoria
Frédéric is sharing with his (expensive) mistress. One should
note how "to the very end of the perspective" explicitly indicates
Flaubert's painterly precision in establishing visual point of
view.

More pervasively, the urban scene as Frédéric takes it in is
broken into fragments or, especially in the nocturnal sightings
to which the novel devotes a good deal of attention, it becomes
something spectral. We shall return to the phenomenon of fragmentation, which anticipates modernist treatments of the city,
but for the moment let me cite a relatively innocent example
that is not thematically fraught. Frédéric, late in the novel, has
been spending the night at the deathbed of M. Dambreuse, the
husband of his wealthy second mistress, and now dawn is ap-
proaching: "They heard, for two hours, the heavy rolling of carts
headed toward Les Halles. The windowpanes whitened, a fiacre
went by, then a herd of she-asses trotting on the pavement, and
hammer blows, cries of street vendors, trumpet bursts; everything was already mingling in the great voice of Paris awakening" (p. 457). The first three verbs here, "heard" *(entendit)*,
"whitened" *(blanchirent)*, and "went by" *(passa)*, are in the historical past, or *passé simple*, the specialized tense generally reserved
for written narratives, but then the verbs disappear altogether
in a succession of sensory data reported as noun phrases, and
when two verbs return, the first is in the imperfect, *trottinaient*
(which I have translated as the present participle "trotting"),
here used to indicate an action sustained through an unspecified
duration, and the second is in the present, *s'éveille* ("awakening"),
to mark cyclical recurrence. I mention the sequence of tenses
because the passage begins with a notation of "historical" narration, the external indicators of the end of the night of vigil

over M. Dambreuse's body, but then turns into a series of disjunct auditory details that are anchored in the as-if-present internal time of the people within the house who hear these
sounds. What is striking is how different this moment is from
Balzac's great catalogues of city sights and sounds, even if it
shares with Balzac a certain excitement over the daily renewal
of vital energies in Paris. There is no urban panorama here as
there is no overviewing narratorial presence. The reality of the
city is intimated as it impinges on the senses of the characters,
and this means that the city is represented not as a whole that
can be grasped metaphorically or otherwise but through synecdoche, through bits and pieces that are connected only by
implication.

Often, moreover, Flaubert subverts the solid grounding in
reality of these fragmentary sensory stimuli by dissolving them
in the fluid medium of the protagonist's fears, fantasies, and
projections. Although the novel begins with a vivid early morning scene—6 A.M., we are told—of a boat's departure, it is noteworthy how frequently Flaubert chooses to give us Frédéric's
vision of the city at night, and in fog. Here he is early in the
book heading back to his rooms after an evening at a restaurant
with his friends:

> Then he went slowly back up the streets. The street lamps
> swayed, making long yellowish reflections tremble over the
> mud. Shadows slipped along the edge of the sidewalks, with
> umbrellas. The pavement was slick, the fog was falling, and it
> seemed to him that the moist shadows enveloping him were
> imperceptibly descending into his heart. (p. 72)

The fact that the other late-night pedestrians are no more
than shadows under umbrellas slipping along the edge of the
sidewalk is of course precisely faithful to Frédéric's visual perspective. At the same time, this solitary walker in the nocturnal
streets imagines these flitting dark images as vaguely menacing,
somehow invading him. Dickens's late, dark masterpiece, *Our*

Mutual Friend, is often cited as a precedent for the representation
of London in *The Waste Land*—Eliot had thought of taking from
it an epigraph for his poem—but that pervasive, disquieting
sense of an "unreal city" is something Eliot might also have
learned from *The Sentimental Education*. Let me offer just one
more brief example out of many. Frédéric, this time in the full
daylight of a midafternoon during which he has been waiting
for Mme Arnoux to appear at the climactic rendezvous to which
she will never come, begins to "pound the pavement" (precisely
the French idiom, *battre le trottoir*) as anything but a flâneur:

> He contemplated the cracks in the pavement, the maws of the
> gutters, the candelabra, the numbers over the doors. The tiniest
> objects became companions for him, or rather ironic spectators;
> and the uniform façades of the houses seemed pitiless to him.
> His feet ached with cold. He felt himself dissolving with the
> sense of being overwhelmed. The reverberation of his footsteps
> shook his brain. (p. 347)

Night and fog are hardly necessary to turn the city into spectral
presences. Frédéric's self-induced inner torment suffices for that.
And the observation of details of the external scene that makes
them "ironic spectators" quickly turns into painful propriocep-
tion—the coldness in the feet, the echoing steps that pound into
the brain.

The Sentimental Education moves back and forth in an intri-
cate dialectic between a beautifully composed painterly whole-
ness of vision and a splintered, also sometimes hallucinatory
view of the world that grasps frenetically or anxiously at disjunct fragments. But the painterly set pieces are never of the
city. In fact, almost all of them focus on Mme Arnoux, seen by
Frédéric through the idealizing medium of romantic projection.
She is typically posed iconographically in interior scenes, sewing
or embroidering or attending to some other domestic or mater-
nal task, at once an image of quiet feminine harmony (her given
name, Marie, triggers the association with representations of the

Madonna) and an exquisite object of desire. Thus Frédéric's initial vision of her sitting in the first-class section of the steamboat, wearing a big straw hat, its pink ribbons fluttering in the
wind behind her, as her dark braids "seemed to press amorously
against the oval of her face" (the seeming is of course the product of Frédéric's desiring gaze) while "her whole figure was
defined [se découpait] against the background of the blue air"
(p. 51) (another elegantly painterly notation, with the blue
linked subliminally to the iconography of the Madonna, who is
usually painted in a blue robe). The counterpoint to these exquisite portraits, which is the mode of representation that dominates the novel, is already evident in the scene on the deck that
immediately precedes Frédéric's first sighting of Mme Arnoux.
Instead of a coherent description of the deck, what we get is a
rapid list of disorderly and sordid fragments—nutshells, cigar
butts, pear skins, leavings of lunches wrapped in greasy paper,
the world outside the frame of the romantically idealized portrait seen as a messy jumble of bits of garbage. The deck of the
steamboat as public space in the opening scene of the novel
offers a model for the vision of the city where the main events
of the book will unfold. Garbage is, of course, one of the principal products of compacted urban life, and in the new cities of
the nineteenth century strategies for the management of the
exponential increase of garbage remained rudimentary, a condition manifested in the vast heap of rubbish that looms over
the London of *Our Mutual Friend*. Garbage, however, is merely
the inert consequence of human activity, and in many of the
street scenes and crowd scenes of *The Sentimental Education*
Flaubert is concerned with evoking his protagonist's perception
of the city in restless motion. The urban panorama, like the
steamboat deck, remains a jumble of glimpsed fragments that
do not hold together, but the fragments are kinetic expressions
of human energies—in the more negative instances these are
the frantically animated cousins of lifeless garbage. This sense
of the city as a compelling arena of incoherence leads to a boldly

innovative mode of representation, anticipating the modernist novel, which we shall go on to explore. Looking ahead to that exploration, I would like to conclude this initial take on Flaubert and the city by quoting one extended passage from the middle section of the novel. Frédéric and Rosanette are coming back in a carriage from a horserace at the Champs de Mars when, in the midst of a sudden downpour, they are caught in a traffic jam on the Champs Elysées:

> From moment to moment, the rows of vehicles, too crowded together, stopped all at once in several lines. Then people were stuck next to each other and inspected each other. From over the edge of the panels with their blazons indifferent looks fell on the crowd; eyes full of envy shone in the depths of the fiacres; disdainful smiles answered proud tilts of the head; wide-open mouths expressed idiotic admiration; and, here and there, some flâneur, in the middle of the road, flung himself backward to evade a horseman galloping between the vehicles and managing to make his way out. Then everything resumed movement: the coachmen loosened the reins, lowered their long whips; the horses, animated, shook their harness chains, tossed foam around them, and the hindquarters and the damp harnesses smoked in the water vapor intersected by the setting sun. Passing under the Arc de Triomphe, it cast a reddish light at a man's height that made the wheel hubs sparkle, the doorknobs, the tips of the team shafts, the saddle rings; and, on both sides of the great avenue—resembling a river in which manes, clothing, human heads undulated—the trees all glistening with rain loomed, like two green walls. The blue sky above came out again in patches, soft as satin. (pp. 271–272)

Like so much in Flaubert, this spectacular scene is, of course, a consciously conceived set piece, and Flaubert cannot resist a certain aestheticizing touch, evident here in the rays of light from the setting sun that cut through the veil of vapor, kindling the shiny surfaces, and in the satin-soft patches of blue sky. But painterly prettiness is by no means the dominant effect of the scene. There could scarcely be a better situation for illustrating the breakdown of community in the modern metropolis, its systemic dysfunction, than a traffic jam. Everyone is trying to get somewhere; everyone is frustrated by all the others who are exasperatingly in the way. In nineteenth-century Paris, class divisions would have played an important role in this clash of frustrations, this isolation of person from person and individual from community. Only the aristocrats and the relatively affluent would have enjoyed the luxury of travel by carriage—those indifferent gazes falling on the crowd from above the carriage panels painted with escutcheons of nobility. There is a certain fit between Flaubertian misanthropy and the social fact of urban anomie as the faces glimpsed in the carriages exhibit pride, envy, disdain, and fawning admiration. The flâneur who makes an incidental appearance in this scene is no longer a vehicle of observation but an object of satiric attention, and, in fact, the chaotic conditions of the crowded street prevent him from exercising his vocation as flâneur, instead force him to leap backward in order to avoid being trampled.

How all this is reported is as important as what is reported. The rather minimal narrative event of a traffic jam after the races is conveyed in the imperfect tense as a continuous experience of indeterminate duration. The report of the scene bears a superficial resemblance to the catalogue of concrete particulars which is one of the trademark devices of the realist novel, but it actually works in an opposite direction. The realist catalogue is a literary warranty of descriptive authority, a strategy for creating the illusion of comprehensiveness on the part of an all-seeing narrator. In the passage we are considering, it is not entirely clear who is doing the seeing. Perhaps it is the protagonist, which is generally the case in this novel, but there are no explicit indications that this is Frédéric's point of view, and perhaps we are to infer that a seamless transition has been effected from the character's perspective to the narrator's. In any case, what the narrative report involves is not steady, lucid overview but a series of *glimpses*—looks from above emblazoned carriage panels, eyes in the depths of fiacres, disdainful smiles and gaping mouths. One could characterize this as description through synecdoche, but it should be noted that there is something slightly disorienting about these disembodied images. The end of the passage, when our gaze is turned to horse rumps and harnesses and sparkling doorknobs, seems somewhat more integrated as a moment of visual perception. The difference may be precisely that this is a fortuitous moment of ephemeral visual harmony when the light from the setting sun cuts through the evaporating mist and pulls together an array of disparate items. Even here, however, the eye of the observer sees disjunct parts in kaleidoscopic motion, with the Champs Elysées likened to "a river in which manes, clothing, human heads undulated."

Flaubert's breakthrough in the representation of the urban realm was to perceive the modern metropolis simultaneously as a locus of powerful, exciting, multifarious stimuli and as a social and spatial reality so vast and inchoately kinetic that it defied taxonomies and thematic definition. The urban crowd as he understood it was the uneasy habitat of the isolate individual—a certain similarity to Dostoevsky's Petersburg suggests itself in this regard—who more often than not saw the others as suspicious, disdainful, or downright spooky. In this setting, the sauntering disengagement of the flâneur was no longer a possibility. The protagonist of *The Sentimental Education* is an existential drifter for whom intensity comes in the vehicle of fantasy rather than through actual experience. This disposition is hardly a product of the modern city but is fostered by it. The mind of this new urban man, grasping shards of sensory data and jagged ends of recollected images, becomes a maelstrom in which the centrifugal elements of experience are whirled together in dizzying combinations. Flaubert's novel marks a moment of transition in which the stylistic unity, the syntactic coherence, and the temporal continuity of realist fiction are preserved while the certitude of realist representation is rejected. The city begins to show a phantasmagoric face, and this version of mid-nineteenth-century Paris looks forward to the menacing masquerade of Bely's *Petersburg*, to the Dublin Night-town scene of Joyce's *Ulysses*, and even to the ghostly trans-mogrification of Prague in Kafka's *The Trial*. But in order to see that affiliation better, we shall have to consider more closely the role of confusion, fantasy, and fragmentation in the experience of the city.

2

Flaubert

Urban Poetics

ONE OF THE CENTRAL expres-
sions of the uncompromising modernism of *The Sentimental Education* is that it is a novel in which nothing really happens. The
short-circuiting of traditional plot is obviously before all else
the consequence of Frédéric's character. He is a person who can
sustain concentration only on his own daydreams, and, unlike
Emma Bovary, he never goes so far as to commit himself to the
catastrophic course of seriously trying to enact the dreams. He
turns round and round the woman he loves and will never possess; he has misdirected affairs with women he ultimately does
not care about; he lives off a modest legacy without ever finding
a vocation; and in the famous ending that reverts to his beginning, he and his friend from boyhood Deslauriers agree that the
best moment of their lives was when as naïve adolescents they
were turned back in mockery from the local brothel, thus leaving their fantasies of splendid erotic fulfillment untarnished by
sordid reality.

All this might seem to argue that the subversion of plot in
The Sentimental Education is a special case, chiefly dictated by
the dysfunctions of the principal character. I would like to pro-

pose, however, that Frédéric's enmeshment in repetition without development, the fissuring of his life experience into direction-less episodes, is strongly coordinated with the nature of the urban world through which he moves as well as with the nature of the political convulsions, at least as Flaubert saw them, man-ifested in the capital city. Traditional narrative—epic, biblical narrative, romance, and the earlier phases of the novel—works on an organizing premise of purposeful continuity. The narrator himself is the underwriter of this continuity, often actually an-nouncing an organizing theme at the beginning, marshaling the characters and events to move through a more or less ordered medium of time to the teleology which is the resolution of the plot, whether tragic or comic. Balzac's discursive narrators, steadily providing us a stream of purportedly instructive infor-mation about the characters, about society, and about human nature as they move their stories forward, are a magisterial manifestation of this assumption of continuity. One event is firmly linked to the next as each social sphere is linked to all the others, while the informing intelligence of the narrator pro-vides an elaborate set of hyperlinks that makes the material of the novel part of an overarching system. It is all this that French critics such as Roland Barthes have in mind when they identify Balzac with what they like to call "the classic novel."

The Flaubert of *Madame Bovary* preserves some sense of allegiance to this premise of continuity. The plot, after all, takes us somewhere, though the developmental trajectory is a down-ward spiral, from the frustrations of provincial married life through the intensifying disappointments of two adulterous af-fairs to the bitterly moralizing tragic ending. In his Parisian novel, Flaubert sets aside all such development just as he largely excludes the vestiges of an authoritative narratorial perspective distinct from the perspective of the characters. The Paris we get here is the Paris that registers itself in Frédéric's eyes and ears and that is filtered through his lucubrations. His perceptions of

the city, as we have already seen, sometimes are strongly colored
by his romantic obsession. Very often, however, they are not
reflections of his psychological peculiarities but on the contrary
are represented as the appropriate, perhaps even inevitable, sensory response to the stimuli showered on him by the urban
milieu. The representation of Paris in *The Sentimental Education*
is very much in line with the new "aesthetic of shock" that Walter Benjamin describes in a memorable passage in his essay on
Baudelaire. Benjamin puts together Baudelaire, the stories of
Poe, the paintings of James Ensor, and a striking statement by
Valéry about the savagery of isolation in the urban crowd, then
connects all these with developments in technology such as the
match, the telephone, photography, and finally film. The new
urban reality, reinforced by its own technological instruments,
isolates the discrete moment, flashing it onto the sensorium,
then rapidly proceeding to the next moment. Traffic (of which
we have observed a spectacular example in Flaubert) is one of
Benjamin's illustrations of the constantly jolting nature of urban
experience: "Moving through this traffic involves the individual
in a series of shocks and collisions. At dangerous intersections,
nervous impulses flow through him like the energy from a
battery."[1]

Benjamin, it should be said, draws on a celebrated essay by
the early-twentieth-century sociologist Georg Simmel, "The
Metropolis and Mental Life." Simmel proposes that the psychology of the new urban person is predicated on "the *intensification of nervous stimulation* [he gives italic emphasis to this
phrase] which results from the swift and uninterrupted change
of outer and inner stimuli." He goes on to suggest that, in contrast to a mind entertaining lasting impressions that "show reg-
ular and habitual contrasts," more consciousness is "used up" in
the denizen of the metropolis by "the rapid crowd of changing
images, the sharp discontinuity in the grasp of a single glance,
and the unexpectedness of onrushing impressions."[2] We shall go

on to observe how richly inventive Flaubert is in devising the
technical means to convey in a literary narrative just such an
experience of a "rapid crowd of changing images."

In precisely this connection, it is worth noticing the kind of
illumination that characteristically defines Flaubert's urban
scenes. (With his consciousness of painterly representation, the
position and nature of light source is often crucial in his artistic
realization of a given scene.) Sometimes the light is wavering
and uncertain; often, instructively, it is stroboscopic, flaring for
a moment and then going out, like the match of which Benjamin
speaks. Such fleeting illumination seen in the streets is precisely
antithetical to the soft, steady lamplight that bathes the perfect
oval of Mme Arnoux's face in those idealized interior scenes.
Early in the novel, Frédéric, at a music hall, meets Mlle Vatnaz,
the *demimondaine* in whose company he will later become ac-
quainted with Rosanette. Her crude lips, heavily rouged, look
almost blood soaked, "but she had striking eyes: tawny with
points of gold in the pupils, full of spirit, love, and sensuality.
They lit up, like lamps, the slightly yellow complexion of her
thin face" (p. 124). There is something weirdly disconcerting as
well as striking in this hyperfocused depiction of tawny eyes
flecked with gold lighting up a sallow face like lamps. A few
moments later, out in the streets, Frédéric actually witnesses
"fireworks, the color of emerald [that] lit up for a moment the
whole garden" (p. 126). Momentary illumination can produce either ephemeral spectacular effects or, as we had occasion to see
earlier, spooky ones. Frédéric, moving on from the fireworks
display, wanders through the late-night streets: "When a pedestrian approached, he tried to distinguish his face. From time to
time, a beam of light passed through the legs, describing an
immense quarter-circle at the level of the pavement; and a man
loomed, in the shadows, with his hod and his lantern" (p. 129).
In this nocturnal encounter in flickering light, the Parisian
street begins to look like a subterranean mineshaft. And just a
few pages farther on, we discover that the fitful illumination of

the city also characterizes Frédéric's purely interior panoramas of thought (in this case, his fantasies about a brilliant legal career): "These images flashed [*fulguraient*], like flares, at the horizon of his life" (p. 139).

The Sentimental Education offers two elaborately wrought extended episodes in which the full experiential sense of the city as a confused theater of disjunct shocks is realized with exemplary brilliance. The first, which one might designate the arena of eros, or debauchery, is the masked ball at which Frédéric meets his future mistress, Rosanette. The second, which is squarely located in the arena of politics, is the series of street scenes that reflect the revolution of 1848. I will begin with the latter because Flaubert's unswerving skepticism about the possibility of meaningful political action is of a piece with his overarching vision of the intersection of urban reality and history and of the loss of human agency in the new urban realm.

Revolution, Parisian style, is enabled by the city. It is the metropolis that harbors concentrations of disaffected masses which can be stirred to rise up against the established order. It is the city streets that can be barricaded to create impromptu bulwarks against the squadrons of attacking government troops. (After 1848 Haussman sought through the broad boulevards he designed to make future barricades more difficult to put up.) Flaubert, by using his disengaged, romantically preoccupied protagonist as the post of observation from which we see the revolution-wracked streets, dissolves political action into incoherent violence. Frédéric is a supreme egoist for whom the revolutionary cause could have no real meaning. Then, as Flaubert surveys one by one the panorama of human types implicated in the revolution, he conveys a sense that his protagonist is not, after all, a special case, for in the perspective of this writer's steely cynicism, no one, however he deludes himself to the contrary, ever transcends his own selfish concerns, and hence revolutionary action in the end is no more than a series of convulsions that change nothing essential, a clash of violent impulses

that is merely the extreme instance of the jangle of conflicting
stimuli which constitutes urban reality. The perceptual unman-
ageability of the city, its resistance to totalizing description, is
mirrored and magnified in the roiling political realm, where the
looked-for large picture splinters into fragmentary images that
discourage a sense of underlying meaning.

It is shrewdly to Flaubert's purpose that he should synchronize a climactic turn in Frédéric's career as lover with the out-
break of the revolution. Mme Arnoux had been on the point of
giving herself to Frédéric, but when she fails to show up for the
portentous rendezvous (unbeknownst to Frédéric, because of her
child's grave illness), he takes Rosanette, with whom he has not
yet been sexually intimate, and on an impulse of vengeance,
escorts her through the violent streets to the love nest he had
prepared for Mme Arnoux.

> By the way of the rue Duphot, they reached the boulevards.
> Japanese lanterns, hanging from the houses, created garlands
> of lights. A confused swarming churned down below; in the
> midst of this shadow, in places, the brightness of bayonets
> shone. A great din was rising. The crowd was too dense, turn-
> ing back was impossible; and they were entering the rue Cau-
> martin when, suddenly, a noise exploded behind them like the
> cracking sound of a huge piece of silk being torn. It was the
> rifle volley of the boulevard des Capucines.
>
> "Ah! They're knocking about some bourgeois," said Frédéric
> tranquilly, for there are situations in which the least cruel of
> men is so detached from others that he could see the human
> race perish without missing a heartbeat. (p. 353)

As everywhere else in Flaubert, the syntax is solid and per-
spicuous and the choice of imagery beautifully precise, but the
overall sense of Paris in the throes of revolution is of a series
of jagged stimuli, rapid shocks to the eye and ear of the observer
who is denied a coherent sense of the whole. Following his usual
practice, Flaubert opens the scene by noting a source of illumination—the Japanese lanterns, evidently swaying in the wind

and describing garlands of lights as they flicker on the retina of
the protagonist. In the shadow scarcely lit by the swaying lanterns, Frédéric can see neither rifles nor soldiers but only, intermittently, the brightness (literally, "whites," *blancheurs*) of bay-
onets. Then he picks up a confusion of sounds, from which the
most suddenly salient one is discriminated, first by its sheer
shock effect, then by the surprising simile of the cracking sound
of torn silk, not only an aestheticizing image—the presence of
silk in the midst of the violence of warfare is certainly startling—but also a means of getting beyond cliché to realize the
actual sound of the rifle volley that Frédéric hears. (Flaubert
himself was actually sitting at a café table at this moment in
1848 barely a hundred yards away when this volley was fired,
perpetrating a notorious massacre. He thought at first that it
was the sound of firecrackers.) The narrator's comment on Frédéric's callous remark is one of the rare moments in *The Sentimental Education* in which he pulls back from the character's
point of view to that characteristically French mode of aphoristic
generalization about human nature which we observed in Balzac.
I would guess that Flaubert felt the disparity between Frédéric's
nonchalant response and the lethal violence of the scene to be
so extreme that it required an uncharacteristic explanatory intervention. But the generalization on the unmoved heart also
offers a recursive perspective on the revolution itself, for the
reader is led to wonder, if this be what the heart really is, what
might be the motives and the actual ends of all those people
killing each other in the streets. In any case, this unusual gesture
of authoritative narratorial discourse highlights through formal
contrast the difference of the language of the preceding paragraph (which is in fact the language of the novel as a whole).
The two share syntactic coherence, but whereas the narrator's
intervention is framed in a timeless present tense of assured
declaration, Frédéric's perception of the revolutionary street is
cast in the imperfect tense of ongoing experience, which is conveyed as a rapid sequence of fragmentary images and sounds.

This repeated process in the novel of a limited perception of transitory images, which are no more than shards of an ungraspable whole, points toward an ultimate vision of the city as phantasmagoria. The very concept, it should be noted, goes back to a mechanical invention introduced at the beginning of the nineteenth century: an exhibition of optical illusions created chiefly by means of a magic lantern. The actual theatrical apparatus of phantasmagoria provides a strong analogue for later novelistic practice. Phantasmagoria is the exact antithesis of the guidebook representation of the city, in which everything can be mapped out, ordered as a social, architectural, and topographical system. In the solvent of phantasmagoria everything is seen as constant disorienting flux, and the lines of division between perception and hallucination, waking and dreaming, blur. In order to gauge the distance Flaubert has moved from Balzac, we should keep in mind the distinction between phantasmagoria and fantasy. That is to say, in Balzac, alongside the elaborately factual inventories of urban milieus that express his realist impulse, there are pronounced elements of fantasy, even when one excludes his forays into the actual fiction of the occult, such as *La peau de chagrin* and *Louis Lambert.* Some critics have spoken of the modern metropolis represented as a version of *The Thousand and One Nights* in the novels of Balzac. As part of his desire to see in Paris the ultimate locus of human energies for evil and for good, as part of the myth of Paris he seeks to create, he populates his books with superheroes, secret societies (the Thirteen), and clandestine settings where arcane rites of eros and power are enacted. All this surely contributes to the sheer fun of reading Balzac, but what it amounts to is the playing out in plot of fantasized images, characters, and events, not a representation of the way the multifaceted reality of the city impinges on the senses of the individual and unlocks underground currents in his psyche. It is this latter procedure, at once a process of rapid perception and free association, that I refer to as phantasmagoria.

One must of course concede that disjunction and disorientation do not in themselves offer a comprehensive description of modern urban experience. The nineteenth-century city could not have been solely a chaos of phantasmagoric fragments. There is in fact an important countervailing direction in the ambitious urban planning of the era, of which Haussman's sweeping and ruthless Parisian renewal project is an exemplary instance. Such impulses to set up geometrically symmetrical networks of broad boulevards and to lay down rectilinear grids manifest a desire to impose rational order and coherent efficiency on urban life. The degree, however, to which this rationalization of the city succeeded was necessarily limited, and one wonders whether it enabled urbanites to perceive space and objects with the easy orderliness to which the planners aspired. The great avenues, in part devised to facilitate the flow of traffic, brought more traffic, more crowding, more disparate stimuli (a consequence still observable in today's cities). And around the rationally plotted urban zones there was an ongoing swarm of demographically dense, discordant, brawling life—as in that planned city of the eighteenth century, Petersburg, where the great *prospekty*, or prospects, laid out by Trezzini were rapidly surrounded by the wretched teeming slums that Dostoevsky evokes in *Crime and Punishment*. With all the rage for order of the urban planners, the new cities retained roiling areas of heterogeneous jumble threatening to transform the cityscape into a screen for phantasmagoria.

Flaubert's great phantasmagoric scene, which, as I have noted, would be picked up by later novelists, is the masked ball. He obviously thought it had considerable importance in the design of his novel because he lavished such attention on its details, devoting some fifteen pages to the scene. The masked ball clearly is meant to be the gateway for Frédéric's entrance into the erotic demimonde of Paris, tapping into the associations of the masquerade or carnival experience with sexual adventure, with the escape from conventionally assigned identities, and with the casting aside of moral and social restraints. But the masked ball is also an extreme and exemplary instance of the distinctive character of urban existence: anonymous individuals, their real nature disguised, encountering one another in a noisy crowd, appetites sharpened and nerves frayed in a dense swirl of provocative and discordant stimuli. (The paintings of Ensor that Benjamin mentions are pointedly relevant to this phenomenon, and a recent cinematic instance, building on a novella of Arthur Schnitzler, is Stanley Kubrick's *Eyes Wide Shut.*) Here is Frédéric, as Rosanette opens the door for him to come into the ball:

> Frédéric was at first dazzled by the lights; he could make out only the silk, the velvet, naked shoulders, a mass of colors that balanced the sounds of an orchestra hidden by greenery, between walls hung in yellow silk, with pastel portraits, here and there, and crystal candelabra in the style of Louis XVI. High lamps, whose frosted globes looked like snowballs, dominated baskets of flowers, set on console tables, in the corners;—and, opposite, after the second, smaller room, one could distinguish, in a third, a bed with twisted columns, possessing a Venetian mirror at its head. (pp. 169–170)

Because the realist novel is to such a large degree about the encounter with new social and moral experience and how it reshapes the protagonist, one of the defining novelistic scenes—a kind of central *topos* of the novel—is the entrance of the protagonist into unfamiliar space. This moment when Frédéric comes into the masked ball has a certain affinity with many scenes in Balzac, especially in its enumeration of details of milieu that characterize the space the protagonist is entering as a distinctive social "habitat"—here, the *grand luxe* of the courtesan with its suggestions of flamboyance, expensive vulgarity, and sensuality. Balzac's general practice, however, is to present such scenes through the narrator's overview, and even in the rare instances when he adopts the character's perspective (as when Lucien de Rubempré in *Lost Illusions* first makes his way into the château of Mme de Bargeton), he maintains a level of formal ordering of exposition which Flaubert deliberately resists. The representation of Frédéric's initial glimpse of the ball and the place where it is set reads like a novelistic anticipation of a cinematic scene done with a hand-held camera. (We will be noting cinematic features in other novels as we go on. Historically, there appears to have been a mutually enriching interplay between the two narrative media: certain practices of the nineteenth-century novel pointed the way for early cinematographers, and in due course film alerted novelists to further refinements of visual representation.) The first notation is, as a reader of Flaubert comes to expect, about the lighting, but from the character's point of view, there are so many bright lights that, instead of clearly distinguishing them, he is "dazzled" by them. (Two complementary verbs that play an important role in *The Sentimental Education* are *éclater*, "to shine brilliantly," or, when applied to sound, "to burst or explode," and *éblouir*, to "dazzle.") In this state of vision momentarily impaired by excessive brightness, Frédéric is at first able to distinguish only disembodied impressions—silk, velvet, naked shoulders—and then finally the discriminated image of the frosted lamp globes. The last clause of the paragraph is a small tour de force in the exhibition of the character's visual and—implicitly—psychological perspective. Standing at the entrance to the main room, one can distinguish (the impersonal *on* is of course Frédéric) a second room, smaller in size, and beyond that, in a direct line, all doors having been left open, the boudoir with its extravagant columned bed dominated by the Venetian mirror. The novelistic *topos* of penetrating unfamiliar space has been, one might say, taken to the second power, as beyond the social space of the ballroom Frédéric gets a sighting of the elegant courtesan's erotic space, a profane sanctum he will fully enter only consid-

erably later in the novel. For the moment, his glimpse of Rosanette's boudoir contributes to the state of erotic excitation in
which he will experience everything at the ball.

All this is not yet phantasmagoria but sets the stage for it.
When a dance begins, "all the women, seated round the room
on benches, stood up in line, briskly; and their skirts, their
scarves, their coiffures began to turn." The unsettling effect of
the novel's relentlessly synecdochic vision is strikingly evident
here: in the crowded ballroom, Frédéric at first sees not women
but skirts, scarves, and coiffures spinning around to the music.

> They were turning so close to him that Frédéric could distin-
> guish the beads of sweat on their foreheads;—and this spinning
> movement, more and more animated and regular, dizzying, con-
> veyed to his mind a kind of intoxication, made other images
> surge up in it, while all of them went by in the same dazzling
> display, each with a special provocation according to the style
> of her beauty. The Polish Girl, who abandoned herself lan-
> guorously, inspired in him the desire to hold her against his
> chest as the two of them glided in a sled over a plain covered
> with snow. Horizons of tranquil sensual delight, on the shore
> of a lake, in a chalet, unfolded beneath the steps of the Swiss
> Girl, who was waltzing with erect torso and lowered eyelids.
> Then, suddenly, the Bacchante, leaning back her brunette head,
> made him think of devouring caresses, in the midst of forests
> of oleanders, in stormy weather, to the confused sound of
> drums. The Fishwife, out of breath from the too rapid beat,
> burst into laughter; and he would have liked, drinking with her
> at the Porcherons, to rumple her neck-scarf with both hands,
> as in the good old days. But the Strumpet, whose nimble toes
> barely grazed the floor, seemed to hide in the suppleness of her
> limbs and in her serious expression all the refinements of mod-
> ern love, which has the precision of science and the mobility of
> a bird. Rosanette was turning, fist on hip; her bob wig, bounc-
> ing on her collar, scattered powdered iris around her, and at
> each turn, with the edge of her golden spurs, she just missed
> catching Frédéric. (pp. 175–176)

There is a double blurring effect here—from the whirling speed of the dance, which is an extreme emblem of the frenetic urban world in which it takes place, and from the hyperkinesis of Frédéric's concupiscent imagination, an imagination kindled by the sense of the metropolis as a vast sexual emporium. The young women in masquerade dress spin by Frédéric in "dazzling display" *(éblouissement)*, triggering in him a state of erotic intoxication. The swiftly shuttling fragmentary images that he actually sees then dissolve into a series of fantasy images which set the different women into different landscapes of desire fulfilled. This mental slide has a certain kinship with Emma Bovary's repeated imaginative flights to horizons of romantic gratification, but it reflects the nature of the crowded urban milieu through which Frédéric moves in being not one sustained erotic reverie but a rapid succession of fragmentary landscapes that, like the movement of the dancers, is *vertigineux*, "dizzying." Even the one phrase that sounds vaguely Balzacian, "all the refinements of modern love, which has the precision of science and the mobility of a bird," is, after all, not an authoritative pronouncement but caught up in the supercharged momentum of Frédéric's point of view, expressing a fantasy about modern love as practiced by the Parisian demimondaine that he will never realize.

The language that Flaubert deploys involves a narrative report, of sorts, but it is clear that the narration of external events and the representation of mental events are thoroughly intertwined, and the sense of duration is as indefinite as in a dream: images succeed one another in time (in the imperfect tense) as Frédéric's mind is swept up in the vertiginous movement of everything around him. The one element of material reality that almost pulls him out of his phantasmagoric haze is that pair of golden spurs Rosanette is wearing, which repeatedly threaten to catch Frédéric's trousers as she goes by, but never do. The act of catching will of course be consummated later in the novel. The golden spurs at this point are a piece of piquant foreshad-

owing that Flaubert the self-conscious artist permits himself,
but the spurs are also elements of a costume and in their very
provocation part of that world of masks which is at once the
arena of the game of desire and of the anonymous urban crowd.
Immersion in this milieu produces a kind of imaginative binge,
a habitual state of the urbanite. Frédéric's mental review of the
night of the ball, as he goes to bed after daybreak, at the very
end of this chapter, precisely reflects the emotional hangover
that follows while pushing to an extreme the process of phantasmagoric fragmentation which we have been following:

> Another thirst had overtaken him, for women, for luxury, and
> for all that constitutes Parisian existence. He felt a little giddy,
> like a man coming off a ship; and in the hallucination of first
> sleep, he saw passing back and forth continually the shoulders
> of the Fishwife, the loins of the Strumpet, the calves of the
> Polish Girl, the hair of the Savage Woman. Then two large
> black eyes, which were not at the ball, appeared; and nimble as
> butterflies, ardent as torches, they came and went, vibrated, rose
> up to the cornice, came down to his mouth. Frédéric strained
> to remember those eyes without success. But the dream had
> already seized him; it seemed to him that he was harnessed at
> Arnoux's to the pole of a fiacre, and that the Marshal, strad-
> dling him, was eviscerating him with her golden spurs.
> (pp. 183–184)

The initial chain which links together women, luxury, and
"all that constitutes Parisian existence" is a small indication that
the masked ball has been conceived as an exemplary instance of
the life of the metropolis, with all its excitements and seductions
and sensory agitation. The comparison of Frédéric's state of
mind to the giddiness of a disembarking sea-voyager reflects an
interest Flaubert shares with the modernists who will follow in
his footsteps in the representation of transitional states of consciousness, between waking and dream, lucidity and hallucination. It has often been observed that the propensity of many
European novelists in the later nineteenth century to conduct

narration through the point of view of the principal character
leads directly to the representation of consciousness through
interior monologue which is the hallmark of a leading current
in modernist fiction. That common formulation could be made
more precise by noting that the line of the novel beginning with
Flaubert and issuing in writers as diverse as Bely, Joyce, Proust,
Kafka, and Faulkner often evinces an interest not just in consciousness as such but in borderline states of consciousness.
What this means is that mental life is not blandly assumed as
an object of representation—like, say, the publishing industry in
Lost Illusions—but is approached as an essentially ambiguous
and perhaps unstable phenomenon. Is consciousness to be conceived as our awareness that we are thinking? Is it the mere
surface expression of murky depths we cannot fathom and do
not control? Does its activity challenge the assumptions of coherence of analytic reason? Is the continuity or integrity of the
self thrown in doubt? Such questions obviously point toward
something like a Freudian model of consciousness, tapping into
a potent unconscious, but as Frédéric's case also illustrates, they
equally reflect the multiform nature of an external, preeminently
urban reality that imposes an overload of stimuli on the expe-
riencing mind.

    In the modernist novel, the lines of demarcation between
different states of consciousness are often deliberately blurred
or altogether erased. Flaubert, working innovatively within the
conventions of nineteenth-century realism, is careful to provide
his readers clear instructions for orientation: Frédéric is "a little
giddy" *(étourdi)*, and the sequence of mental images belongs to
"the hallucination of first sleep." Nevertheless, there is a compelling continuity between the character of the dream images
that appear to Frédéric and what he took in with waking eyes
at the ball. In both instances, vision is fractured into the perception of disjunct fragments. In the dream, this process as-
sumes a certain violence, as female body parts float across the
screen of the mind; so that one is unsure whether to call this

an erotic dream or an erotic nightmare. The disembodied black
eyes that flutter up to the ceiling then down to Frédéric's mouth
are of course the eyes of Mme Arnoux, though in the dream he
himself suppresses the recognition. Their appearance here after
the shoulders and loins and calves of the demimondaines from
the ball dislodges Mme Arnoux from that domestic frame of the
Madonna-like portraits and puts her into play in a wilder erotic
zone. Does the butterfly image suggest her elusiveness and the
fluttering around his mouth his unadmitted sense of her as a
sexual tease? In any case, as Frédéric slips into a deeper level
of dreaming ("But the dream had already seized him"), his focus
switches from Mme Arnoux to the woman who is her antithesis,
Rosanette, identified here as the Marshal, the costume persona
she adopted for the ball. This concluding image of the dream,
and of the chapter, is truly nightmarish, unless one prefers to
regard it as a masochist's wish-fulfillment dream: Rosanette (at
the home of Arnoux, her current lover) astride Frédéric, dis-
emboweling him with those all-too-well-remembered golden
spurs. Flaubert, in his commitment to a faithful rendering of the
violent contradictions of the mind, pushes the limits here of the
decorum of nineteenth-century fiction. The real nature of modern love may not be the precision of science and the mobility of
a bird, as the waking Frédéric imagined, but rather addiction,
subjugation, and the painful destruction of the self. Within the
novel, the lurid image of a bespurred Rosanette straddling Frédéric may point forward to a sadomasochistic undercurrent in
the relationship between them that ensues, for though there is
no indication that she explicitly plays the role of dominatrix
toward him, as she does in the dream, his affair with her, seemingly a sensible solution to sexual and social needs, is in fact
the negation of his romantic dreams and a disastrous thwarting
of the superior self he aspires to be. Beyond this particular novel,
Rosanette as murderous sexual equestrian is a vivid anticipation of the many modernist representations of the mind at war
with itself, shaken by dark impulses of perversion and self-

destruction. Half a century later, she will have a memorable avatar in Bella Cohen, the whorehouse madam of *Ulysses*, who, transformed into a man in the phantasmagoria of the Nighttown episode, will bestride a feminized Leopold Bloom, whip him, and pour on him a torrent of verbal abuse.

Flaubert's exquisitely wrought language stands as a splendid bridge between two literary eras. The large project of the nineteenth-century novel had been to bring readers the news (as the English name for the genre suggests) about contemporary life. The exemplary manifestation of that project was Balzac's *Human Comedy*, with its flaunted aspiration to a comprehensive description of French society. The impulse was to be shared by Zola and, across the Channel, in a different manner, by Thackeray, George Eliot, and Trollope—the title he chose for one of his books, *The Way We Live Now*, precisely reflects this ambition of contemporary reporting enacted by many of the novelists of the age. (Dickens poses a complicated special case that deserves attention in its own right.) Bringing the news entails a certain stylistic clarity: the narrator in one way or another must take the reader in hand for the proposed tour through the labyrinth of contemporary society. Flaubert does not reject the prevailing norm of stylistic coherence, even in this, his most radical novel, but he sets aside the ambition to convey to readers the news about society both because he does not consider that a realizable aim, given the nature of both history and the new urban reality, and because he does not find it something particularly interesting to do. In any case, the unflagging syntactic lucidity and the tensile cohesiveness of his prose owe as much to his desire to make language a polished artifact as to any implicit contract of communication with his readers. He grandly announced in one of his letters that he sought to create a new order of prose that would take over the high literary functions of poetry. One of the things he had in mind was an expressive rhythmic perfection in prose writing, coordinated with a fine-tuned orchestration of images, and this characteristic is continually observable in the style of *The Sen-timental Education*. But I also suspect that Flaubert, like his great twentieth-century admirer Nabokov, thought of poetry as a ve-hicle for the manifestation of precision—perhaps even a preci-sion greater than that of science. Thus he joins the tightly cinched units of a lucid syntax with the most remarkable im-pulse of lexical specification. Flaubert has the exact word for all the minute material realities of the urban milieu—the details of architectural ornamentation and furniture, the sundry elements of fashionable attire, the contents of the shops, the various com-ponent parts of carriages and harnesses. Because his narration is to a large extent taken up with such details observed sequen-tially by the protagonist, figurative language, of which he is a great master, plays a relatively limited role. With few excep-tions, the occasional metaphors and similes do not aestheticize the objects to which they refer but, on the contrary, add a nuance of precision, like the comparison of gunfire to the sound of ripped silk, or the likening of the surge of a mob of rioters to "a river stemmed by an equinoctial tide."

But this continual sequence of material details produces nothing like a Balzacian report. The rhythms of the prose are very often staccato as the narrator conveys to us in little syn-tactic bundles strung out in sequence the objects that come into Frédéric's field of vision which are the flotsam and jetsam of an intensely kinetic, disruptive reality intrinsically resistant to co-herent comprehension. It is precisely for this reason that the orgiastic scene of the masked ball and the revolutionary violence in the streets are the exemplary instances of Flaubert's imagi-nation of Paris. If one asks why Flaubert chose to set his Pa-risian novel two decades earlier than the time of writing, it is in part so that he could synchronize historically Frédéric's love for Mme Arnoux with his own love for her model, Elisa Schles-inger, but, more significantly, because he wanted to place his inveterately disengaged protagonist in Paris in the eye of the historical storm of 1848, a storm that fully realized the potential

for vehement disorder of the modern city. Let me cite a last
brief example of how this prose is fashioned to render this sense
of reality. These are the concluding sentences of a description—
as always, through Frédéric's eyes—of a private house in the
vicinity of the Panthéon ravaged by the street battles:

> Awnings, held by a nail, hung like rags. The stairs had col-
> lapsed, doors opened on the void. One could make out the in-
> terior of rooms with their papers in shreds; delicate objects had
> been kept there, once upon a time. Frédéric observed a grand-
> father clock, a parrot's perch, some prints. (p. 408)

The syntactic bundling of successive perceptions—awnings,
stairs, doors, interiors—characteristic of the novel as a whole is
prominent here. It is also characteristic, even in many scenes
quite unrelated to revolutionary violence, that what the eye
takes in is mostly tag ends and shards of things. The only sign
here of figurative language is barely that, for the awnings that
"hung like rags" have in fact been reduced to rags. In the parade
of objects perceived, the nature of the perceiving consciousness
is elliptically conveyed in the bit of narrated monologue, surely
Frédéric's wry unspoken reflection, "delicate objects had been
kept there, once upon a time." But the feeling of the moment is
powerfully communicated by the bare sequential report, without
comment, of what the character sees: "a grandfather clock, a
parrot's perch, some prints." These objects are not meant to be
what Roland Barthes called a "reality effect," serving merely to
signify the category of the real—in any case, a problematic concept—but, rather, eloquently express both a whole high-
bourgeois realm ravaged by the revolution and Frédéric's response, at once acidic and impotent, to the destruction.

Throughout the novel, as a direct consequence of the narrative technique of experiential realism embodied in its language, the urban world is never represented in and of itself but
always through the sensibility, the preoccupations, and the limited visual or auditory vantage point of the protagonist, with

easy crossovers from external objects and events to purely mental events, some of them sheer fantasy. The city is solidly there
as a central fact of social and historical reality, but this narrative
approach to it may suggest that its distinctive character can be
represented only through the ways in which it impinges on a
particular consciousness and perhaps reinforces or even shapes
a particular cast of mind. The great city, with its shifting crowd
of isolates (a term Melville seizes on etymologically in its Span-
ish form at the beginning of *Moby-Dick* in speaking of the island-
dwelling inhabitants of Manhattan), is a breeding ground for
fantasy and fragmentary perception. By and large, this mode of
perception is fraught with menace for Flaubert, though there
are other writers who would take it as an occasion for exuberance, a liberating mode of apprehension through which the mind
might revel in the sheer teeming multifariousness of urban experience. The seeds of the stream of consciousness, a narrative
technique especially suited for registering response to the multifarious and discontinuous realities of the modern metropolis,
are already evident in Flaubert's rendering of these sequences
of discrete, often disoriented, observations by Frédéric Moreau.
It will require just another step in literary evolution and a further shift in historical experience to move from the formal prec-
edents set by this novel to Leopold Bloom wandering through
the streets of Dublin and Clarissa Dalloway looking out the
window at the passing panorama of London. For this beginning
point of the story of the novel's response to the modern city, it
suffices to say that Flaubert, without overtly rewriting the prevailing conventions of the genre, had succeeded in fashioning
an innovative language that could register the compelling, disturbing, and essentially centrifugal character of the new urban
realm.

3

Dickens

The Realism of Metaphor

IN TRACING A LINE FROM Flaubert's extraordinary innovations in rendering the city through the protagonist's perspective to the interior monologues of the modernist novel, one runs the risk of assuming a kind of evolutionary model for the history of the novel. In such a view, the fussiness of high-profile omniscient narration and the confidence of an objective report of external reality are sloughed off as the novel fully realizes its vocation of persuasively representing subjective experience. There is, however, only a partial and therefore misleading truth in such a linear account. Sundry modes of authoritative narration have continued to appeal to many writers, from Flaubert's time down to ours. Zola had greeted *The Sentimental Education* with an enthusiastic review in 1869, but *La curée* (The chase), the first novel in his vast Rougon-Macquart series, which he published two years later, owes far more to Balzac than to Flaubert. The rhetorically flaunted authority of the Balzacian narrator is eliminated by Zola, but the impressive image of Paris he builds in the novel to a large extent rests on the careful depiction of solid material realities—elaborate, sometimes extravagant, catalogues of interior décors and clothing worn and vehicles ridden in and the façades of houses. His Paris of the Second Empire, an age of urban renewal and rampant shady speculation in real estate, is given strong thematic definition, not as in Balzac through the narrator's pronouncements but through the emphatically selective details of the plot, in which everything is made to turn on the twin motives of cupidity and concupiscence. The overview of the changing metropolis produced through this method can be riveting in its scenic concreteness—for example, the panorama of urban demolition as part of Haussman's grand project near the end of the novel—and in the force of its judgmental perspective. What is lacking is that keen sense of the subjective feel of quotidian experience in the new urban reality which Flaubert was so successful in conveying. In any case, the solidity of the external world continued to engage novelists after Zola, not only among his French, English, and American followers conventionally labeled Naturalists, but even down to some of our own contemporaries (Tom Wolfe, a self-conscious throwback, may be a dubious example; much of John Updike is a strong instance). What has become clear, eight decades after the peak years of High Modernism, is that the radical interiorization of narrative variously realized by some of the modernists has proved to be not a grand culmination of the novel as a genre but rather a great moment of compelling innovation, after which novelists have gone their sundry ways, a few of them building on the modernist formal precedent, a good many others ignoring it.

No novelist of the nineteenth century could serve better than Dickens to dislodge linear conceptions of the development of the novel. His gifts and his writing procedures are in most respects precisely antithetical to those of Flaubert. (Among the modernists, Joyce and Kafka would find very different ways to assimilate elements from both.) Whereas Flaubert wrote with meticulous slowness, painstakingly revising, and virtually invented the so-called art novel, Dickens wrote at breakneck speed for serial publication, brilliantly improvising. Though his concern with the problematic character of contemporary urban reality—a concern manifested in the works of few other Victorian novelists—progressively deepened, he never ceased to see himself as a popular entertainer. (Revealingly, in *Hard Times* he uses the circus as his analogue for the realm of the imagination opposed to the grim utilitarianism of the nineteenth-century industrial world.) Even in his darker late novels, he was clearly compelled by a sense that his audience must be amused—amused by the vivacious chatter and the playful formal apostrophes of the narrator, surely somewhat old-fashioned by the 1860s, amused by the management of suspense, the surprising turns of plot, the comic-grotesque characters, the happy endings accompanied by a vigorous administering of poetic justice to the villains (at the end of *Our Mutual Friend*, one of them is actually trundled off in a wheelbarrow). If one major direction in the development of the novel is a process of interiorization, it must be said that Dickens adheres quite unswervingly to an external and omniscient point of view. He is so far from inviting us to see the world through the character's eyes that when he slips into doing so for a few lines at the beginning of chapter 19 of *Barnaby Rudge*, he feels obliged to apologize: "for which apt comparison the historian may by no means take any credit to himself, the same being the invention . . . of the chaste and modest Miggs, who . . . did, in her maiden meditation, give utterance to the simile."

Yet Dickens was acutely aware that he was writing about a London in the throes of drastic and perhaps ominous transformation, and he was able increasingly to deploy his distinctive imaginative resources in a consistently external mode of narration to convey the feel of life in this new urban reality. The process of rapid expansion—largely through immigration from the provinces, with the introduction of new technologies and a terrific compaction of urban population, which we have observed in Paris—is palpable in contemporaneous London on a more awesome scale. The population of London in 1800 was about a million; by midcentury, it had swelled to 2,320,000, a slightly faster rate of growth than that of Paris; by the end of the century, it almost tripled again, reaching 6,480,000. Unlike Paris on the Seine, London on the much larger Thames was a bustling port city, the hub of the most extensive international commerce, as we are reminded in the plot of *Dombey and Son,* which ships off one of its heroes, young Walter, to distant seas. It was also a vast city, almost ten times larger than Paris in physical area, and this vastness is a feature that Dickens occasionally represents, as we shall see, in panoramic overview. If the Parisian of this era seems to have had a sense of being jostled and jolted by an overabundance of sensory stimuli, this condition was compounded for the Londoner by a feeling of being dwarfed by the cityscape and sometimes menaced by the material products of compacted urban existence. The visual prospect from above of London, shown in some photographs from the period, was a wilderness of smokestacks and chimney pots. In this era before central heating, each principal room (in the best of circumstances) had its own fireplace, burning soft coal, especially conducive to pollution, with the annual consumption of coal for the city reaching an astounding total of 3.5 million tons. Dickens's prose, especially in his last completed novel, *Our Mutual Friend* (1864–1865), profoundly registered the consequences of this ecological menace both for the individual living in the city and for the collective urban population.

He was, as many testimonies by his contemporaries suggest, a passionate Londoner. All his life, he loved exploring London's nooks and crannies, usually on foot, undeterred by the filth and stench and threat of disease of its slums, and he could amaze his friends with his minute knowledge of its most obscure neighborhoods and byways. But if Dickens the man might have been in some ways the London equivalent of a Parisian flâneur, there is nothing of the flâneur in the perspectives on the city that his narrators offer us. He has the mapped coordinates of the city firmly in mind, as some of the details of orientation he provides his readers show, but he is up to something very different from cartography. Here is a fleeting instance from *Our Mutual Friend* that may serve as an introduction to the more elaborate deployment of Dickens's peculiar and compelling vision of the urban world. First the careful geographic indication: the two characters, the grim schoolmaster Bradley Headstone and his obsequious disciple Charley Hexam, have crossed Westminster Bridge from the Surrey side and are walking "along the Middlesex shore towards Millbank." "In this region," the narrator continues, "are a certain little street, called Church Street, and a certain little square, called Smith Square, in the centre of which last retreat is a very hideous church with four towers at the four corners, generally resembling some petrified monster, frightful and gigantic, on its back, with its legs in the air."[1] This striking image, which is given no further development and bears no obvious general thematic weight, is as gratuitous as it is wonderful. Many readers have noticed a fairy-tale perspective in Dickens's writing by virtue of which monsters, ogres, and other supernatural creatures suddenly manifest themselves, usually through the agency of figurative language, in the most mundane contemporary settings. I would by no means gainsay the presence of fairy-tale elements in this fictional world, but I would prefer to give that notion a little more edge by suggesting that Dickens repeatedly exercises a faculty of *archaic vision* in which what meets the eye in the contemporary scene triggers certain primal fears and fantasies, archaic vision becoming the medium through which we are led to see the troubling meanings of the new urban reality. In the example just quoted, a piece of ugly and pretentious architecture is transformed into a menacing monster. The manifest intention is satire in the grotesque mode, but the effect is to induce a certain anxiety (in the reader, not the characters) about the disjunction between human observer and the inhuman monstrosity of the external world, in this case a building. The four-legged monster on its back is of a piece with the fantasized presence of a great dinosaur in the dense London fog that hangs over the famous beginning of *Bleak House*, where, as in *Moby-Dick*, the evolutionary-primeval and the biblical-primeval are casually intertwined: "As much mud in the streets, as if the waters had but newly retired from the face of the earth, and it would not be wonderful to meet Megalosaurus, forty feet long or so, waddling like an elephantine lizard up Holburn-hill."[2]

The key to Dickens's searching vision of the cityscape is his use of figurative language. After Shakespeare, he is probably the greatest master of metaphor in the English language. The originality and fecundity of his metaphoric imagination constitute one of the chief reasons that he is a law unto himself as a novelist, with no really convincing imitators. Balzac's metaphors by comparison are conventional, serving, as we have seen, the linked purposes of hyperbole and allegory. Dickens's metaphors and similes are vividly original, often startling, and give the impression of having been struck off in the white heat of improvisation. The local effect of the metaphor is frequently quite brilliant while, especially in his elaborate descriptive set pieces, which he typically places at the beginnings of chapters and books, there is much densely interwoven unity of recurring image and theme. I suspect that Dickens did not altogether plan such unity—certainly not the way that Joyce, with his colored pencils and charts, mapped out the network of motifs for *Ulysses*—but rather was carried along by the powerful momentum of his integrative imagination.

Let us first consider an instance of a simile that has a strictly local function. The narrator of *Our Mutual Friend* is describing the neighborhood, at the meeting point of Kent and Surrey, where Bradley Headstone's school and a companion school for girls are located:

They were in a neighborhood which looked like a toy neighborhood taken in blocks out of a box by a child of particularly incoherent mind, and set up anyhow; here, one side of a new street; there, a large solitary public-house facing nowhere; here, another unfinished street already in ruins; there, a church; here, an immense new warehouse; there, a dilapidated old country villa; then, a medley of black ditch, sparkling cucumber-frame, rank field, richly cultivated garden, brick viaduct, arch-spanned canal, and disorder of frowsiness and fog. As if the child had given the table a kick and gone to sleep. (p. 218)

The messy architectural and functional promiscuity of this scene of urban transition is aptly caught in the long catalogue of contradictory structures, the strident "medley" that includes both black ditch and sparkling cucumber frame and duly registers the presence of formations dictated by the new technology, such as the brick viaduct and the arch-spanned canal. Catalogues of this sort, of course, are a staple of nineteenth-century realism, and in fact they figure prominently in the panorama of urban demolition in Zola's *The Chase* to which I have referred. A small clue to the Dickensian difference in the handling of the realist catalogue may be detected in the flaunted paradox of "another unfinished street already in ruins" (behind which could lie a subliminal memory of Job 3:14, which reads, in the King James Version, "With kings and counselors of the earth, which build desolate places [more literally, "ruins"] for themselves"). What makes the crucial difference, however, is the framing of the catalogue by the simile of the mad and capricious child. That comparison is, one may assume, meant to be whimsically satirical at the expense of the new urban scene, but what it also intimates is an unsettling loss of agency in the rapid transformation of the metropolis. Change takes place helter-skelter, without purposeful direction. A new street is laid out alongside vacancies; another turns into ruins without ever having been completed; a solitary pub stares into nowhere; and the structures of faith and trade are mismatched neighbors. In all this, the notion of an urban community with a coherent collective purpose dissolves. One of the central contradictions of Dickens's achievement is that it is so thoroughly of its Victorian age and at the same time anticipates thematically and sometimes even technically modernist practices in fiction and in poetry. This simile of the deranged child actually has a precise counterpart in Kafka, when K., the protagonist of *The Castle*, looks up at the incoherent structure of the castle on the hilltop and imagines that it might have been flung together by a mad child. Although Kafka, as we know, was an attentive reader of Dickens, it is not clear that he was familiar with this particular novel, so I am not suggesting a borrowing, only what may be an instructive affinity. Among the modernists, Kafka was the assiduous explorer of ontological and epistemological disjunction between the individual and the social, institutional, and topographical reality in which he struggled to insert himself. Dickens surely has not reached such an extreme place. The cosiness and cheeriness of the Dickensian world are quite genuine, and he continues to imagine in novel after novel a small sustaining community of the kindhearted within the urban wasteland. Nevertheless, his sense of the expanding city in the new industrial age as human purpose tumbling out of control, sliding into blind incoherence, points forward toward some of the bleaker visions of the modernists.

This sense of a loss of control, of being surrounded by menacing and perhaps inscrutable entities, is nicely appropriate for the detective-novel aspects of Dickens, in *Our Mutual Friend* and elsewhere. Here is a particularly arresting moment, when the two young lawyers, Eugene Wrayburn and Mortimer Lightfoot, accompanied by a police inspector, glide along the Thames at daybreak in the boat of the sinister Rogue Riderhood, in search of the body of Gaffer Hexam:

> They were all shivering, and everything about them seemed to be shivering; the river itself, craft, rigging, sails, such early smoke as there yet was on shore. Black with wet, and altered to the eye by white patches of hail and sleet, the huddled buildings looked lower than usual, as if they were cowering, and had shrunk from the cold. Very little life was to be seen on either

bank, windows and doors were shut, and the staring black and white letters upon wharves and warehouses "looked," said Eugene to Mortimer, "like inscriptions over the graves of dead businesses."

As they glided slowly on, keeping under the shore, and sneaking in and out among the shipping, by back-alleys of water, in a pilfering way that seemed to be their boatman's normal manner of progression, all the objects among which they crept were so huge in contrast to their wretched boat as to threaten to crush it. Not a ship's hull, with its rusty iron links of cable run out of hawse-holes long discoloured with the iron's rusty tears, but seemed to be there with a fell intention. Not a figurehead but had the menacing look of bursting forward to run them down. Not a sluice-gate, or a painted scale upon a wall, showing the depth of water, but seemed to hint, like that dreadfully facetious Wolf in bed in Grandmamma's cottage, "That's to drown *you* in, my dears!" Not a lumbering black barge, with its cracked and blistered side impending over them, but seemed to suck at the river with a thirst for sucking them under. And everything so vaunted the spoiling influences of water—discoloured copper, rotten wood, honey-combed stone, dank green deposit—that the after-consequences of being crushed, sucked under, and drawn down, looked as ugly to the imagination as the main event. (pp. 171–172)

The precision of observed material details, strikingly confirmed by contemporaneous photographs of the scene along the Thames, is extraordinary, but everything is manifestly observed from a peculiar and powerfully transforming point of view. The sense of menace in the setting is of course what is felt by the men in the boat, and this is as close as Dickens comes to adopting the perspective of his characters, as one can see when Wrayburn's remark about inscriptions over the graves of dead businesses confirms the general view of the riverbank that the narrator is conveying. It is the narrator, nevertheless, who remains prominently in charge of the presentation, taking in with his authoritative overview the shivering men as well as the seemingly shivering river, craft, and rigging, animating, in characteristic Dickensian fashion, the inert buildings as cowering creatures shrinking from the cold. The disparity in scale between the three men in the boat (Riderhood, their boatsman, presumably would have a different perspective) and the tangle of vast maritime objects they pass is both specific to this tense narrative moment and generalizable to the predicament of the human being—anything but a riverine flâneur—in the iron immensity and decaying jumble of the cityscape.

The apparition of Little Red Riding Hood at the heart of this grim scene is a Dickensian signature. What Dickens profoundly understands about fairy tales is not chiefly that they have happy endings but that they express, as Bruno Bettleheim would stress, the primal fears of the helpless child. If there is a note of jocularity in citing the big bad wolf, it is a nervous jocularity, for what the invocation of Little Red Riding Hood's story is meant to remind us is that there are savage creatures out there that are waiting to eat us all up, that the Thames setting is as scary as the woods in the old tale.

This terror of engulfment is powerfully coordinated with a recurring central theme of the novel and vividly illustrates what I have called the integrative power of Dickens's imagination. The plot of this book spectacularly turns on death by drowning (still another reason why T. S. Eliot initially thought to use a quotation from it as an epigraph for *The Waste Land*). In the opening scene Gaffer Hexam, assisted by his daughter Lizzie, fishes a corpse out of the Thames. He himself is destined to become another such drowned corpse. The protagonist, John Harmon, is generally assumed to have died by drowning, a fate he narrowly escapes and from which he is resurrected, as Eugene Wrayburn will be late in the novel, while the two villains of differing class and temperament, Headstone and Riderhood, will perish in the shallow water of a canal lock, fiercely clasped together. Death stalks the city in much of the later Dickens, beginning with *Bleak House,* and in *Our Mutual Friend* its principal conduit is the Thames, the very waterway that carries the teeming commercial life of the city which is reflected in our passage in the long prospect of looming ships. In this journey on the Thames in the bleak light of a rainy wintry dawn, everything in the extravagantly personified setting has the look of threatening to drown the observer: not only the river but also the structures of the ships and barges and of the wharves seem poised to pull a person down into the watery depths. All this, as we have just noted, points toward the thematic center of the novel. Given the hovering ambiguity about the point of view from which this menacing scene is represented, the pervasive threat of drowning could be limited to the three passengers in the boat or could be taken to address any sentient being making its way through this aqueous urban landscape of iron, rust, and rot. The Thames itself, in the very midst of its function as a vehicle of modern commerce, is associated in the book with a primal muck of dissolution that is indifferent to all human values (another manifestation of Dickens's archaic vision). This association is fixed at the very beginning of the book in the scene with Gaffer in his scavenger boat on the river. His boat is "allied to the bottom of the river rather than to its surface by reason of the slime and ooze with which it was covered," and he himself, in garments "seeming to be made out of the mud that begrimed his boat" (pp. 2, 3), is less a member of any recognizably human society than a troglodyte of the modern urban zone of savagery.

Dickens as a novelist of the city reveals a certain surprising affinity with his ostensibly antithetical contemporary, Flaubert. *The Sentimental Education*, as we have seen, is an elegantly crafted seismograph of the bewildering shocks of modern urban experience and of the individual's concomitant sense of loss of direction and meaningful human connection in the flux of the urban crowd. On the surface, the Dickensian world could scarcely be more different. It is shaped through brilliant improvisation with very little in the way of elegant technical crafting, and the writer exhibits scant interest in representing experience through the eyes of the individual character. According to one popular preconception, Dickens celebrates the colorful variety of his London metropolitan setting: in any case, as a novelist who uses a steadily authoritative overviewing narrator, he has no concern with, and indeed no technical access to, that essentially disorienting shower of multifarious stimuli which is the hallmark of urban experience in Flaubert. Nevertheless, Dickens shares with Flaubert an imaginative intuition that the rapidly expanding metropolis—in the case of London, we might recall, expanding by a factor of more than six during the century in which Dickens wrote—was running out of control. Both writers have a sense that the very dimensions of the modern city dwarf the individual, threaten to subvert the exercise of human agency. Flaubert, faithful to the representational bias of the experiential realism that he perfected, registers this predicament as a perceptual problem, a confusion of individual consciousness. Dickens, deploying with great virtuosity a series of panoramic views of the city, is drawn by the terrific energy of his own metaphoric inventiveness to weave images of the new urban world that raise questions about its viability as an embodiment of human civilization, that interrogate it not from the point of view of the individual but from that of humankind collectively. At just this moment, many hundred miles to the east, Dostoevsky, who was a keen reader of both Flaubert and Dickens, though with a greater imaginative kinship with the English writer, was articulating a vision of Petersburg that combined both these perspectives: in *Crime and Punishment* (1866), the filth, disorder, and oppressiveness of the city are repeatedly seen from Raskolnikov's fevered point of view, but there is also an implicit overview of the modern city as something that objectively has become a site of social and moral pathology.

We rightly think of Dickens as a dedicated reformist, a lifelong believer in the possibility of ameliorating social conditions through conscientious effort. This is another respect in which he is a polar opposite to Flaubert, who came to a globally cynical

view of politics and of society's capacity to transcend the clash
of inveterate egoisms in order to effect positive change. In keeping with this contrast, Dickens was able to imagine affection
and community as Flaubert never did, but one should also note
that his representation of human solidarity characteristically se-
questers it in protected little enclaves within the larger urban
scene, such as the weird patch of pastoral island on the rooftop
inhabited by the doll's dressmaker, Jenny Wren, and her oddly
assorted friends. But beyond these dreams of loving community
and beyond the commitment to reformist optimism, the expanse
of the city in the later Dickens is repeatedly, and powerfully,
envisioned as a theater of chaos and dissolution.

One useful way to see how he deploys this troubled view is
to attend to his visual treatment of the city. Both Dickens and
Flaubert are intensely visual novelists, but in drastically different ways. Flaubert is so beautifully precise in representing how
the character's eye picks up elements of the world that impinges
on it that his novels have often been taken, with considerable
justification, as precursors to the subjective camera in cinema.
(Frédéric's vision of the kaleidoscope of the masked ball whirling
around him, which we looked at in detail, is one exemplary instance among many.) Dickens, on the other hand, perhaps somewhat surprisingly, proves to be protocinematic in his own quite
different way. In an instructive essay of the 1930s, Sergei Eisenstein, the great Russian director, proposes that Dickens's visual handling of crowd scenes, with rapid cutting from one clus-
ter of images to the next, was a strong anticipation of montage
technique upon which the early filmmakers directly drew. Eisenstein analyzes the beginning of chapter 21 of *Oliver Twist* as
a deployment of montage, then cites a brief passage from *Hard
Times* about the bleak sameness of daily routine in Coketown as
an instance of Dickens's "out-distancing Hollywood's picture of
the city by eighty years."[3] Eisenstein's testimony is helpful,
whether or not Dickens was actually a direct source for early
film editing, because it reminds us that this writer's represen-

tations of the city exhibit great technical virtuosity, often visually focused, even in the absence of technical calculation.

A central case in point is the Dickensian treatment of material clutter in the Victorian city. This is a great age of material accumulation on the part of the affluent classes, largely enabled and certainly accelerated by the Industrial Revolution. That combined economic and technological development, not incidentally, spewed out a vast profusion of manufactured objects together with the waste products of industrial process, with all such objects and waste products then densely crowding the space, both outside and inside, inhabited by city dwellers. Now the realist catalogue of objects, a novelistic procedure that we have already noted in passing, is an enduring literary testimony to the nineteenth century as an age of clutter. The catalogue, however, as it is typically managed by Balzac or Zola, is actually an *ordering* device. The long list of material items creates an illusion of comprehensive representation, but in fact the details almost always reflect an interpretive bias of selection, and through the seeming welter of details the writer is providing sociological, thematic, even psychological definition of the milieu and of the characters that belong to it. The later Dickens, by contrast, begins to view clutter as a more ominous and uncontrollable phenomenon that does not allow itself to become the vehicle of confident narratorial interpretation. There is something ultimately illegible about urban existence for Dickens, as Efraim Sicher properly emphasizes in his recent comprehensive study of the Dickensian representation of the city: "No description could convey the totality of the city, so Dickens proceeds by negation, by describing the failure to describe, or by giving us catalogues of disconnected objects which disturb us in their unexpected and absurd combination."[4] In *Bleak House*, spectacularly, the overwhelming accumulation of scraps and oddments of Mr. Krook's rag and bottle warehouse engenders spontaneous combustion, a correlative to the choked institutions of the law that may have no egress except through conflagration. *Our Mu-*

tual Friend depicts a grotesque first cousin to Krook's warehouse in the bizarre jumble of Mr. Venus's taxidermy shop (from which Hitchcock surely picked up something for his comic-macabre filming of the taxidermist's in *The Thirty-nine Steps*), but the novel's more salient representation of clutter is as piled up filth, in the looming presence of Harmon's dust heap, from which wealth is extracted, and in the rain of pollution on the city, to which, as we shall see, this book devotes a good deal of attention.

Here is one of many set pieces on the subject of dirt. The ostensible narrative context is a dinner shared by Wrayburn and Lightwood in a Thameside cottage they are renting, but the narrator's overview of a windswept spring evening has little to do, notwithstanding his pretence to the contrary, with the perspective of the two young men at table together.

The grating wind sawed rather than blew; and as it sawed, the sawdust swirled about the sawpit. Every street was a sawpit, and there were no top sawyers; every passenger was an under-sawyer, with the sawdust blinding him and choking him.

That mysterious paper currency which circulates in London when the wind blows, gyrated here and there and everywhere. Whence can it come, whither can it go? It hangs on every bush, flutters in every tree, is caught by the electric wires, haunts every enclosure, drinks at every pump, cowers at every grating, shudders upon every plot of grass, seeks rest in vain behind the legions of iron rails. In Paris, where nothing is wasted, costly and luxurious city though it be, but where wonderful human ants creep out of holes and pick up every scrap, there is no such thing. There, it blows nothing but dust. There, sharp eyes and sharp stomachs reap even the east wind, and get something out of it.

The wind sawed, and the sawdust whirled. The shrubs wrung their many hands, bemoaning that they had been over-persuaded by the sun to bud; the young leaves pined; the sparrows repented of their early marriages, like men and women; the colours of the rainbow were discernible, not in the floral spring, but in the faces of the people whom it nibbled and pinched. And ever the wind sawed, and the sawdust whirled.

When the spring evenings are too long and light to shut
out, and such weather is rife, the city which Mr. Podsnap ex-
planatorily called London, Londres, London, is at its worst.
Such a black shrill city, combining the qualities of a smokey
house and a scolding wife; such a gritty city; such a hopeless
city, with no rent in the leaden canopy of its sky; such a belea-
guered city; invested by the great Marsh Forces of Essex and
Kent. (pp. 144–145).

Dickens deploys one of his favorite rhetorical strategies here.
He strikes a metaphor—the grating wind as an immense saw—
and runs with it, turning the wind-driven litter blowing through
the streets into sawdust and London itself into a vast sawpit,
insisting through anaphora on his metaphoric terms, converting
his initial statement of the metaphor into a virtual refrain: "And
ever the wind sawed, and the sawdust whirled." The metaphor
neatly conveys the abrasive, noisy effect of the wind, and it is
appropriate to the urban setting that it is a metaphor drawn
from an industrial process which gives off an irritating waste
product. It is notably an industrial or craft process that has run
out of control: there is no top-sawyer—according to the *Oxford
English Dictionary*, a term that originally referred to the person
working the upper handle of a pit saw—only under-sawyers in
the pit, choked and blinded by sawdust. (From *Bleak House* onward, Dickens repeatedly registers a concern that the London
atmosphere was, both literally and figuratively, becoming un-
breathable. This is an apprehension of the city in *Our Mutual
Friend* that we shall have occasion to pursue in greater detail.)
The central metaphor, I would suggest, has a paradoxical double
effect. It takes over the scene, as we have been observing, but
it does not diminish, and may even sharpen, the visual representation of the scene. As with a panning camera, our view is
carried over the streets of the city, following the whirl of paper
waste around gratings, iron rails, pumps, lawns, enclosures, and
electric wires (this last detail, which refers to telegraph wires,
is evidence of a relatively new technology in the mid-nineteenth

century). Whether the contrasting switch to Paris—which I suspect Eisenstein would identify as a bit of montage—is historically accurate, it works well enough as a rhetorical antithesis to this characterization of London. At the same time, it might invite the reader to a double take, for precisely what is going on in London in the attempted exploitation of Harmon's dust heap and in the scavenging of corpses from the Thames is an activity of human ants with sharp eyes and sharp stomachs pouncing on every scrap. The metaphoric equation of garbage and money has a distinctly disorienting effect: superimposed on the image of a London littered with refuse is an image of "currency" fluttering all over the cityscape, imparting a sense of the unseemliness, the worthlessness, of the very thing universally pursued.

Another characteristic feature of the passage and of Dickens in general is the slide from witty conceit to dire perspectives that transcend the satiric playfulness of the occasion. The shrubs wringing their many hands, like other fairy-tale touches in Dickens's flaunted personifications, have something incipiently nightmarish about them. The sparrows that repent of their early marriages, "like men and women," suggest a rather dim view of youthful romantic illusion, not exactly compatible with the blissful unions through which Dickens ties up his happy endings, while at the same time they raise the spooky prospect of the whole fecund order of nature undone in the city. The conceit about the rainbow colors of the pinched faces is a bit of rhetorically flaunted paradox, but it also reminds us of something merely implicit till now, that the cityscape under the slate sky is utterly drained of color. London itself, finally, the "black shrill city" under "the leaden canopy of its sky," becomes the subject of figurative transformation, is said to combine aspects of "a smokey house" (all those chimney pots) and "a scolding wife" (perhaps a carryover from those early marriages that are to be regretted).

The direness of what might at first seem merely a vivid

evocation of an annoyance, a harsh wind blowing litter and grit,
is reinforced by a couple of biblical echoes in the prose. The
scavengers who "reap even the east wind" recall Hosea 8:7, "For
they have sown the wind, and they shall reap the whirlwind,"
while the east wind itself repeatedly figures in the Bible—for
example, in the plagues narrative in Exodus—as the bearer of
desolation. The rhetorical question about the wind, "Whence can
it come, whither can it go?" uses archaizing language that is in
all likelihood inspired by the King James Version, pointing toward an associative link with the image of the futilely circling
wind in the first chapter of Ecclesiastes: "It whirleth about continually, and the wind returneth again according to his circuits."
Surely the bleak sense in Ecclesiastes of a wind that goes round
and round to no purpose or profit is a fitting backdrop for the
wind here blowing through contemporary London.

Finally, since Dickens not only elaborates metaphors with
great resourcefulness but also proliferates metaphors, it should
be noted that the central figure of litter as sawdust is complicated by the figure of litter as "paper currency." There is probably an etymological pun involved because "currency" is that
which goes around. Paper currency is something that has no
intrinsic worth but is taken to represent worth. Ostensibly no
more than a witty throwaway on the part of the narrator, the
phrase engages the economic dimension of the production of
urban waste that is central to *Our Mutual Friend*. Those who
are fond of such identifications, as some interpreters of this
novel have been, may choose to introduce the Freudian equation
between money and feces. Dickens himself seems more focused
on the denial of human value in what is most valued in a society
held together by the cash nexus. Money is garbage. Like accu-
mulated garbage, it chokes out life. The churning mills and
grinding saws and smoking chimneys of the modern commercial
city produce vast mounds of garbage, and from these somehow
wealth is extracted. In all this, I am not sure whether Dickens
exhibits any adequate sense of productive labor (his virtuous

characters rarely appear to do any meaningful work) or of how industry, for all its manifest abuses and deleterious consequences, might be enabling a collective existence beyond the subsistence level of preindustrial societies. What he did see with the greatest penetration was how crowded urban life in the industrial age had become alarmingly clogged and polluted by its own material products. This is a perception he succeeded in conveying in his later novels not abstractly or didactically but with imagistic concreteness and often even with a kind of kinesthetic immediacy. In the vastness of the new metropolis as he powerfully evoked it, men and women were gasping for air, starving for the sunlight that was hidden behind the leaden canopy which sealed the city in a claustrophobic prison. We shall now go on to consider the full encompassing reach of Dickens's ecological vision.

4

Dickens

Intimations of Apocalypse

THE TREATMENT OF THE CITY in the novels of Dickens evolves through time, not in an entirely consistent chronological trajectory but nevertheless with a noticeable difference in emphasis after he reaches the height of his powers. It is that evolution which justifies for our purposes concentrating on the later Dickens and in particular on his last completed novel. He was, of course, fascinated with London from the start, but in the earlier novels the fascination manifests itself chiefly in an activity of scrupulous observation intertwined with lively, sometimes fantastic caricature. This makes his narrator roughly analogous to Balzac's curious and knowledgeable narrator-flâneur, though with a fondness for the humorous and the grotesque unlike Balzac. What does not much engage his imagination in the early books is a desire to convey the palpable changing feel of collective experience in the new metropolis or a sense that the city was being rapidly transformed into a qualitatively different kind of space. The early Dickens is of course perfectly aware that London is not only a lively bustling place but also a dangerous one. Yet the slums and urban crime are hardly a new phenomenon of the modern metropolis, and London had had its Fagins and Bill Sykeses for centuries. The point at which Dickens begins to evince in his fiction a perception of London in the throes of momentous historical change is in *Dombey and Son* (1846). The focus of the change in this book is the invasion of the city by the railway, and the long passage in which he evokes the architectural and commercial upheaval of Stagg's Gardens effected by the introduction of the railway is justly famous. Speed, energy, the rushing movement of crowds are all associated here with this new technology. Dickens contemplates the locomotives themselves with mingled apprehension and excitement as "tame dragons" that make "the walls quake, as if they were dilating with the secret knowledge of great powers yet unsuspected in them, and strong purposes not yet achieved." In regard to the altered sense of human life in the new industrial city energized and dominated by the railway, Dickens shrewdly zeroes in on the idea of how time is measured. He shows us a cityscape stocked with "railway plans, maps, views, . . . and timetables," traversed by members of Parliament "with their watches in their hands," where "railway time [was] observed in clocks, as if the sun itself had given in."[1] It was in fact railway timetables that led to a general adoption of precise, mechanically measured time and impelled people with the wherewithal to begin to carry around pocket watches so that they could check at any moment where they stood in relation to an objective, minutely calibrated temporal grid. (Carrying around these precise portable chronometric devices altered a person's relation to time in a way analogous to the revolution in communication effected in our own age by the introduction of the mobile phone.) Spring-action mechanical clocks had been around since the fifteenth century, but the first clocks that offered more than a rough approximation of time were the pendulum clocks invented in the mid-seventeenth century, and these were not exactly portable items. An extremely precise watch was invented in 1761 for the purposes of navigation. Such watches could hardly have been generally available over the next few decades, but the introduction of railway transportation gave an impetus to their wide-spread use. Six years after Dickens wrote this passage, Greenwich Mean Time would be initiated, a further testimony to the need of modern technologies for precise standardized time. Before the railway, people by and large continued to gauge time as they always had, by the sun, the very apprehension of temporality thus being determined by the diurnal rhythm of the natural world. Dickens keenly understands that the railway introduces a transposition of a fundamental category of our experience from the realm of nature to that of human calculation and technology. All this is behind the rapidly tossed off phrase, "as if the sun itself had given in." Within a few years, first in *Bleak House* and then in *Our Mutual Friend*, this idea of the sun's giving in will carry still graver implications.

The railway passages of *Dombey and Son* are the exception rather than the rule in that novel, which is far less concerned with the phenomenology of the new urban existence than with a moral drama—or if you will, melodrama—about the desiccation of human feeling under the dispensation of contemporary commercialism. Most of Dickens's formidable descriptive energies are lavished here not on urban panoramas but on interior scenes, where he can exhibit through details of décor, sometimes demonically possessed, the freezing of emotions in the domicile of the mercantile magnate Mr. Dombey. And in the street scenes that we do get, what predominates is the sense of vivid and grotesque life in the animated bustle of catalogues of details, as in the earlier novels. Similar procedures are much in evidence in *Little Dorrit*, nine years after *Dombey and Son*, and are probably dictated by the fact that the action of that novel is set in a London three decades before the time of writing.

It is in *Bleak House* (1852–1853) that Dickens first spectacularly exercises a troubled panoramic vision of human existence in the new metropolis. The celebrated opening passage on the London fog is of course a piece of bravura writing that establishes what amounts to a symbolic atmosphere for the novel

(another formal anticipation by Dickens of a modernist procedure), making the dirty fog a meteorological correlative for the
suffocating obfuscation of British legal institutions that is the
chief context of the action. What is most remarkable about the
fog of these initial paragraphs, however, is not that it is symbolic, not that it is rhetorically displayed with the grand insistence of anaphora that Dickens used with such virtuosity, but
that it is so precisely observed. The urban phenomenon that
arrests the novelist's attention, as it will even more in *Our Mutual Friend*, is pollution, and the appalling black fog he describes
is really what we would call smog: "Smoke lowering down from
chimney-pots, making a soft black drizzle, with flakes of soot in
it as big as full-grown snowflakes—gone into mourning, one
might imagine, for the death of the sun."[2] The death of the sun
here is a scarier notion than the giving in of the sun in *Dombey*.
In a manner characteristic of the later Dickens, it is a half-
joking, fanciful conceit that triggers somber implications far in
excess of the play of wit ostensibly intended in the conceit. The
sun seems to have died because it is nowhere visible in this
smog-enveloped cityscape. But what the eye of the observer
picks up is the gravest reversal of the order of nature—flakes
of soot, produced by all that burning coal, flutter down instead
of snowflakes, as though nature were wearing mourning, and,
in the logic of the image, the sun is not merely hidden by the
smog but extinct. Though introduced as a kind of nervous joke,
the death of the sun is no laughing matter: the very phrase is
part of our culture's primary language for apocalyptic endings,
from the biblical prophets (compare Jeremiah 4:23: "I beheld the
earth, and, lo, it was without form, and void; and the heavens,
and they had no light") and the Book of Revelation to modern
science fiction.

Dickens, it should be said, does not make these momentary
apocalyptic imaginings integral to what happens in the novel.
In *Bleak House* the furthest he will go in intimating a force of
dissolution working through contemporary society is to suggest

that the disease bred in the filthy slum of Tom-all-alone's will spread to the most privileged precincts. This idea is in part didactic remonstration, as the tones of moral castigation invoked clearly show: "There is not an atom of Tom's slime, not a cubic inch of any pestilential gas in which he lives, not one obscenity or degradation about him, not an ignorance, not a wickedness, not a brutality of his committing, but shall work its retribution, through every order of society, up to the proudest of the proud, and to the highest of the high" (pp. 654, 657). (The typhus epidemics that ravaged London in the middle decades of the century are very much on Dickens's mind, and his reference to "pestilential gas" appears to adopt the so-called miasmatic theory of contagion that was then current, though he is also using the spread of disease from low class to high as an emblem of the process by which the exploitation and neglect of the disadvantaged will eat away at the foundations of society as a whole.) Jo from the wretched filth of Tom-all-alone's as a bearer of contagion that will touch the houses of the rich also manifests a mechanism of Dickensian plot, a feature that in relation to the eighteenth-century novel has been amusingly called, in a phrase borrowed from Fielding, "the law of conservation of character"; in these elaborately plotted books of Dickens's, the very antithesis of *The Sentimental Education*, almost no character is allowed to go to waste; each somehow is linked with the others as the writer deftly brings all the strands together in the complication and resolution of the story. It is worth noting both the didactic impulse and the formal necessity because there is, I think, a certain disjunction between the conventionalism of Dickens's plots and of his moral exhortations and the depth of perception opened up by his powerful metaphorical imagination, to which we shall now attend in *Our Mutual Friend*.

What does metaphor have to do with the language of the novel that we have been keeping in view? The single feature that most distinguishes novelistic narration from other kinds of narration, from epic to romance to folktale, is its intrinsic, and

often spectacularly displayed, formal fluidity. Narration in a
novel can rapidly glide back and forth from grand overviews to
the restricted and emotionally colored view of a single character. It can adopt, as we saw in Flaubert, the spatial and temporal orientation of a fictional personage with a technical sub-
tlety and conviction matched by no other narrative genre. It
can segue from the report of action to lengthy essayistic reflection, as novelists from Fielding to Proust and Musil have done
to a variety of different purposes. This freedom of the novelistic
narrator to do more or less anything he wants is also manifested in the deployment of figurative language. Metaphor,
which for convenience sake I shall conflate here with simile, is
of course an available resource in any mode of narration. In
narrative genres other than the novel, it by and large plays an
ancillary role in relation to narration proper, highlighting or
focusing the narrative events. This is basically how Flaubert
uses it, sparingly, in *Madame Bovary,* whereas in *The Sentimental
Education,* as I have noted, what little figuration occurs is limited to giving more vivid definition to sensory data. Even the
extended simile of Homeric epic is a formally contained device,
introducing an elaborately performed pause in the forward rush
of narration, providing visual realization for the act or object to
which it refers, and, in the case of the *Iliad,* creating a window
from the realm of war into some scene from quotidian peaceful
existence. Figuration can also be used that way in novelistic
narration, but, given the formal license of the genre, it often is
not a contained device but quite the opposite—a vehicle of inventive association that spills over and rolls on, as Proust's
similes do in one way and Dickens's in another. Figurative language thus deployed becomes an instrument of discovery, and
the very notion that metaphor is background and narration is
foreground is called into question, for what happens in the
novel, thematically, perceptually, philosophically, may occur as
much through the spinning out of metaphor as in what one
character does or says to another. Metaphor as a primary ve-

hicle for novelistic imagination is what one sees again and again in Dickens, and perhaps with growing force in the later novels.

The hallmark of the Dickensian simile is that it exercises a power seemingly in excess of the occasion for which it is introduced that proves, on reflection, to be eerily warranted. This process is observable even in relatively brief local metaphors clearly intended for comic effect. Thus Alfred Lammle, the frustrated fortune hunter, is seen "engaged in a deed of violence with a bottle of soda-water, as though he were wringing the neck of some unlucky creature and pouring its blood down his throat."[3] This image makes the failed sharp-dealer look very foolish indeed, and as a way of putting a petty villain in his place, it is quite funny. At the same time, I think that in reading we duly register the vehemently macabre character of the simile. This penny-ante scoundrel is not going to commit any murder in the novel, but in his rage at being thwarted in his schemes, he is boiling with murderous impulses that are wonderfully revealed in his deed of violence against the bottle and in the hypothetical conversion of soda water to blood and hence man to vampire. The sheer extravagance of the image in this fashion turns out to accord psychological penetration into the character. Dickens uses figurative language precisely to this purpose, though much more extensively, in representing an actually murderous, and tormented, villain, Bradley Headstone. What I should now like to consider is how this extraordinary energy of figuration enables a particular vision of nineteenth-century London in the novel.

Early in the book, Lizzie Hexam, after sending off her brother Charley to become Headstone's assistant, stands at the open door looking out over the Thames in the light of dawn. Her standing there, at any rate, is the formal occasion for the view provided, though nothing in the language appears to owe anything to her consciousness, the verbal performance being very much the narrator's:

> The white face of the winter day came sluggishly on, veiled in
> a frosty mist; and the shadowy ships in the river slowly changed
> to black substances; and the sun, blood-red on the eastern
> marshes behind dark masts and yards, seemed filled with the
> ruins of a forest it had set on fire. (p. 74)

In part, this striking perspective can be explained as "at-
mospheric" writing, though of a very high order. That is, when-
ever we are in the proximity of Gaffer Hexam (who will appear
in the next paragraph) or Rogue Riderhood and the louche
Thameside hangouts they frequent, the evocation of the scene
introduces sinister or ominous overtones, with intimations of
violence lurking in the shadows. The language, however, has a
force that carries beyond the effect of mere suspenseful atmosphere. London, at this early morning hour swathed in mist
rather than in impenetrable smog, dissolves into a Baudelairean
"unreal city." (It is no doubt only fortuitous that the three great
nineteenth-century metropolises often subjected to novelistic
scrutiny—London, Paris, and Petersburg—were all, having
been built along marshlands, prone to fog, encouraging novelists
to see them as spectral apparitions.) Dickens, even when he is
not rhetorically exhibiting explicit metaphors, is often busy
imagining his subject metaphorically. Here, the winter day is
personified as possessing a "white face" covered with a veil, with
the frosty whiteness then set off by the black profiles of the
shadowy ships and the blood-red of the rising sun. It is with
the appearance of the sun that a more explicit metaphor surfaces,
mingling the substances of blood and fire in a palpably infernal
vision of the city. The antithesis between nature and the constructed human world, never far from Dickens's imagination, is
powerfully brought forward in the image of the red disk of the
rising sun as a backdrop for the tangle of masts and yards of
the anchored ships: all those were once part of a growing forest;
now seen against the sun, they seem once more like a forest,
but one caught in flame. It is important, of course, to preserve

a sense of proportion in noting such moments in Dickens. He is not, after all, a voice prophesying doom. Nevertheless, the momentum of his metaphoric imagination unsettles our sense of the city as a solid, substantial theater for the realization of the collective designs of human will. Hellfires intermittently flicker on his colorful and sometimes quite engaging urban horizon. The city is often seen as a departure from, or even a violation of, the order of nature, and in the deepest reach of his metaphoric imagination he evinces certain forebodings as to the price that may be exacted for this alienation from the natural world.

Our Mutual Friend moves back and forth among three iconic urban settings which are intricately linked by image and theme. These are the Thames (an instance of which we have just observed), with its contiguous slums; the financial district (the City of London in the restrictive sense of the name); and the rather vaguely indicated neighborhood dominated by the looming Harmon dust heap. The moments when Dickens offers metaphoric overviews of the cityscape generally occur, as I observed earlier, at or very near the beginning of chapters, the overview providing a scenic and thematic introduction to the action about to unfold, and this will be the case for all of the passages we shall consider. Let us first look at two coordinated takes on the City of London, placed at a considerable distance from each other in the text (respectively, the beginning of book III, chapter 16, and near the beginning of book II, chapter 15). Here is the City as Bella Wilfer heads to her father's countinghouse, where she and her father and John Harmon will have a delightful private supper—another instance of a little pastoral asylum within the grim urban setting:

> The City looked unpromising enough, as Bella made her way along its gritty streets. Most of its money-mills were slackening sail, or had left off grinding for the day. The master-millers had already departed, and the journeymen were departing. There was a jaded aspect on the business lanes and courts, and the very pavements had a weary appearance, confused by the tread

of a million feet. There must be hours of night to temper down
the day's distraction of so feverish a place. As yet the worry of
the newly-stopped whirling and grinding on the part of the
money-mills seemed to linger in the air, and the quiet was more
like the prostration of a spent giant than of one who was re-
newing his strength. (p. 603)

Although the controlling metaphor here is, at least for Dickens, a relatively conventional one, a good deal of imaginative
work is going on through its articulation. "Money-mill" may be
a cliché, but Dickens makes the milling powerfully pervade the
passage. The streets through which Bella walks are realistically
"gritty" because of the prevailing pollution, but grit of course
comprises the fine abrasive particles produced by some sort of
grinding action, and so a quasi-causal, metaphorical connection
is set up between the grittiness of the streets and the daily
grinding of the money mills. (The causal link is not entirely
fanciful because if London were not a great center of commerce,
it would not have its terrific concentration of population—"the
tread of a million feet"—and without that population, it would
not be plagued by pollution.) Nineteenth-century London, of
course, is not primarily an industrial city but rather a commercial one. The image of mills superimposed on the financial district intimates the intrinsic connection between industry and
finance, even though it particularly invokes windmills. (In the
playing out of the metaphor here, there is a certain deliberate
blurring between the older technology of windmills and modern
industry.) The image also suggests that the exhausting, dehumanizing labor in the clanging iron setting of the factory has a
close equivalent for those who push papers in the counting-
houses instead of working machines. The giant at the end of the
passage, token of the huge power of the commercial center, is
another of those Dickensian gestures toward fairy tale, though
it may also register a subliminal recollection of *Don Quixote*,
since the money mills are, after all, figured as windmills ("slack-
ening sail"). In any case, "spent" for "exhausted" in the final

clause makes a neatly summarizing pun: exhausted energies are renewed through rest, but this giant is spent, like money, which once disbursed is simply gone. The daily cycle of grinding out profits at feverish pace is a "distraction" of the human spirit, depleting its resources with scant promise of replenishment, subverting the bond between humanity and the sustaining order of nature.

A view of the City of London earlier in the novel is still grimmer, perhaps because it is a prelude to the appearance of that dour man of self-manacling iron, Bradley Headstone. It, too, exhibits grit and grinding:

> A grey dusty withered evening in London city has not a hopeful aspect. The closed warehouses and offices have an air of death about them, and the national dread of colour has an air of mourning. The towers and steeples of the many house-encompassed churches, dark and dingy as the sky that seems descending on them, are no relief to the general gloom; a sundial on a church-wall has the look, in its useless black shade, of having failed in its business enterprise and stopped payment for ever; melancholy waifs and strays of housekeepers and porters sweep melancholy waifs and strays of papers and pins into the kennels, and other more melancholy waifs explore them, searching and stooping and poking for anything to sell. The set of humanity outward from the City is as a set of prisoners departing from a gaol, and dismal Newgate seems quite as fit a stronghold for the mighty Lord Mayor as his own state-dwelling.
>
> On such an evening, when the City grit gets into the hair and eyes and skin, and when the fallen leaves of the few unhappy City trees grind down in corners under wheels of wind, the schoolmaster and his pupil emerged upon the Leadenhall Street region, spying eastward for Lizzie. (p. 393)

The visionary power of Dickens's integrative imagination is especially evident here. The evening sky is covered with clouds; the indication that they are "dingy" is another of those constant suggestions in the novel of dirt and pollution.[4] The idea that the sky "seems descending" on the houses conveys a sense of claustral enclosure, for the city feels cut off from the wide world of nature, and this claustral sense prepares the way for the figure of imprisonment at the end of the paragraph. In this instance, Dickens does not use the device of anaphora to which he is so attached, but he nevertheless imparts a unity of thematic perspective by lining up a whole set of overlapping, nearly synonymous attributes. The sequence "grey dusty withered" leads quickly to "death," semantically echoed in "an air of mourning" and "black shade," visually reinforced by "dark and dingy," with the integrated effect of the whole underlined phonetically by the alliteration: dusty-death-dark-dingy-descending-departing-dismal. There are four elaborated metaphors here that manage to hang together effectively: first death, then bankruptcy (which is commercial death), then the swept away refuse as strays and waifs, then incarceration. The repetition of melancholy waifs and strays sweeping away melancholy waifs and strays of refuse to be picked through by other human counterparts takes up the novel's recurrent sense of all economic activity as an unending chain of scavenging, wealth extracted from garbage. The fact that the street people are poking through the refuse takes us back to the defining first scene of the novel, in which Gaffer Hexam poles the Thames in search of human bodies and whatever of worth they may carry. Marxists may happily find here an image of alienated labor, Foucauldians an image of the carceral self. What is clear is that Dickens's vision of capitalist society at the height of the Industrial Revolution discerns in all the new distortions of human relations not productive labor but instead an endless dirty paper chase, filthy lucre extracted from filth.

The heart of this extraordinary constellation of metaphor is the fantastically witty representation of the sundial as having gone into bankruptcy. This is an especially ingenious and resonant deployment of the recurrent Dickensian idea of the death of the sun. The sundial cannot indicate time, of course, because

the sky is covered with dingy clouds. The metaphor of bankruptcy is metonymically triggered by the sundial's location in
the financial district. The fact that it is set into a church wall,
which is realistically plausible, provides a quiet intimation of the
futility or irrelevance of religion in this dead urban world of
finance. The metaphor is at once amusing and ominous (a distinctively late-Dickensian combination), for a sundial that has
"stopped payment for ever" is a forlorn, now useless, index of
time in a world hopelessly estranged from nature where it seems
as though the sun will never shine again. For a fleeting moment,
as though in stroboscopic illumination generated by the incan-
descence of the metaphor, the great modern commercial city is
seen as a dark arena of cosmic catastrophe, its inhabitants reduced to pathetic dung beetles or hopeless prisoners, exiled from
the world of life-giving light. Then, as the narrator slides down
from urban panorama to a close-up of his two characters, the
grim aspect of the evening modulates to mere irritation, that
grit which penetrates hair and eyes and skin.

The last extended instance of Dickens's vision of London
that we shall consider pushes all these themes a step further. It
is also the most panoramic urban view that the novel offers,
moving from the outlying countryside to what the narrator himself calls "the heart of the City":

It was a foggy day in London, and the fog was heavy and dark.
Animate London, with smarting eyes and irritated lungs, was
blinking, wheezing, and choking; inanimate London was a sooty
spectre, divided in purpose between being visible and invisible,
and so being wholly neither. Gaslights flared in the shops with
a haggard and unblest air, as knowing themselves to be night-
creatures that had no business abroad under the sun; while the
sun itself, when it was for a few minutes dimly indicated
through circling eddies of fog, showed as if it had gone out,
and were collapsing flat and cold. Even in the surrounding
country it was a foggy day, but there the fog was grey, whereas
in London it was, at about the boundary line, dark yellow, and

a little within it brown, and then browner, and then browner, until at the heart of the City—which call Saint Mary Axe—it was rusty-black. From any point of the high ridge of land northward, it might have been discerned that the loftiest buildings made an occasional struggle to get their heads above the foggy sea, and especially that the great dome of Saint Paul's seemed to die hard; but this was not perceivable in the streets at their feet, where the whole metropolis was a heap of vapour charged with muffled sound of wheels, and enfolding a gigantic catarrh. (p. 420)

As an evocation of London fog, this passage is still more precise and perhaps even more thematically complicated that the familiar fog passage at the beginning of *Bleak House*. It vividly demonstrates that a mode of representation which may still be justifiably called realism is perfectly compatible with the exercise of what might be thought of as a faculty of visionary fantasy enabled by metaphor. The fusion of these two kinds of writing also calls into question the accuracy of that all-purpose concept, omniscient narration. Balzac's narrators, as we had occasion to observe earlier, are omniscient in the precise sense that they flaunt their knowledge, setting themselves up as both quasi-scientific authorities on the contemporary world with all its institutions and as moral guides to the workings of the human heart. The Dickensian narrator we see in action here is omniscient in the more limited sense that he abundantly exploits great mobility of visual perspective—zooming in on the wheezing pedestrians and the flaring gaslamps inside the shops, scooting out to the countryside, inviting us to see what "might have been discerned" "from any point of the high ridge of land northward," then diving back down to join the perspective of people in the streets. At the same time, he chooses to see in the scene he reports through his elaborately figurative language not just the scene itself but what it might be in the process of ultimately becoming. He appears to do this, moreover, not from the standpoint of a detached, and protected, observer but from that of someone taking part with visceral immediacy in the collective experience he is observing.

The precision of observation is impressive. This is as good a description as one could want of the differential citywide distribution of smog in nineteenth-century London. The narrator's panoramic view moves inward through concentric circles from the still unpolluted fog in the countryside—which figures in the plot of the novel as a place of regeneration—to the yellow-tinged fog near the city limits to the poisonous brown and reddish-black smog of the metropolitan center that looks rather like modern Los Angeles on a very bad day. All this is done with that rich orchestration of related terms and images, that semantic density of synonymity, which Dickens is able to achieve repeatedly in the midst of rapid improvisation. (Even the visually precise "rusty-black" at the heart of the City may pick up its rust associatively from the near-to-hand iron tool in "Saint Mary Axe.")

Dickens is also faithful to visual experience in representing the city enveloped by fog, hovering between visibility and invisibility, as possessing a spectral appearance—a notion, we noted, that occurs in Flaubert's Paris, from the subjective viewpoint of the protagonist, and that will pervade Bely's *Petersburg*, as we shall have occasion to see. In Dickens, however, the visual phantasmagoric is quickly transformed into a thematic phantasmagoric. Having designated inanimate London "a sooty spectre," the narrator proceeds to invoke a disturbing world of spooks. The opposition between the animate and the inanimate city etymologically reminds us that these are ostensibly the realm inhabited by a living spirit, *anima*, and the realm devoid of it; but, as elsewhere, Dickens works the ambiguities of connection and correspondence between these two seemingly opposed categories. Fog-enshrouded London, like a ghost, cannot make up its mind whether to be visible or not; and the gaslamps, which in a right order of things should be lit at night, not in the daytime, turn into spooks, "night-creatures," "with a haggard and unblest air."

Now a ghost is an intermediate creature between the living and the dead, and as such it coordinates nicely with the two salient physiological images here of a transitional state between life and death—choking and drowning. The choking and wheezing are of course the direct bodily response to severe pollution (the sort of day when contemporary authorities warn people with pulmonary disorders to stay indoors), and so they may be said to participate in the realism of the passage. The brilliantly hideous metaphor of the "gigantic catarrh" at the very end of the paragraph focuses this collective experience of respiratory difficulties, also reinforcing the notions of rheumy fluids, bleariness, and messiness—all that the industrial age has made of London in Dickens's eyes. The gigantic catarrh enfolded in the city equally links up with the more lethal interference with breathing involved in drowning. The representation of the whole city drowning in fog (lofty Saint Paul's the last to go) of course carries forward the images of death by drowning that run through the novel from that first somber scene on the Thames to the death of Rogue Riderhood and Bradley Headstone in the canal lock near the end. Asphyxiation, under water or above, is a kind of inner drowning, and thus the actual physiological response to the smog of choking and wheezing and the figuration of the smog as an engulfing sea are physically synchronized events.

The heart of the passage and of Dickens's darkest imaginings about the modern city is the image of the death of the sun, which we have considered in other contexts. Once again, there is a striking continuity between visual precision and visionary fantastication. In the represented scene, the sun is for the most part effectively hidden or at least neutralized in its brightness by the dense layer of brown and rusty-black smog. When it becomes fleetingly visible, it appears as a wan, flat disk, shorn of its power to warm and light up the world. But the way Dickens puts this, in one of his arresting images based on a hypothetical condition, is that it "showed as if it had gone out, and were collapsing flat and cold." This seems to me a grimmer evocation of the extinguishing of the sun than the nervous jocularity of the bankrupt-sundial image: what follows the "as if" is a chilling sense of light dying in the universe. Dickens may well have in mind, as Michael Cotsell proposes, Laplace's "nebular hypothesis" about the eventual cooling of the sun, but he has integrated it into his own poetic world.[5]

It is not easy to say how such apocalyptic perspectives should be taken. They occur, of course, in a novel abounding in comic elements, where the villains will in due course get their just deserts and the virtuous souls will live happily ever after, enveloped in cosy good feeling. But a work of literature is, among other things, a highly complex mnemonic apparatus. Images, ideas, and events, once introduced, even in a subjunctive mode indicating a condition contrary to fact, are retained in circulation in the world of the text. In Dickens's imagination, the pall of smog over the great city is not just a nuisance, not even just a threat to the health of the city dwellers. Pastoral remains an important point of reference for his conception of things, which is to say, the idea of a harmonious vital bond between humankind and nature. The city in the industrial age spells the irrevocable end of the pastoral prospect—at least in Dickens's understanding, though we shall see that Virginia Woolf tries to hang on to some sort of pastoral vision. The barrier of pollution that insulates the metropolis from nature is dense with the ominous idea that the modern city—in its terrific concentration of population, its runaway production of noxious waste products, its frenetic dedication to the accumulation of wealth—could prove to be, in the worst of possible projections, an irreversible catastrophe for human existence on this globe.

This is, one must admit, a rather drastic way of stating the implications of a series of fleeting images in Dickens's late novels. I don't mean to suggest that these apocalyptic images convey the ultimate "truth" about the city as he saw it. The precipitously expanding London of his era was a place of over-crowding, wretched slums, moneygrubbing, and appalling pollution, but it also exhibited, as his novels attest, the allure of teeming human variety and of driving energies. In the 1860s, few steps had been taken to alleviate the encroaching ecological disaster that Dickens, and many of his contemporaries, saw. Yet in this very period, when urban planning was being put into practice in many cities across Europe and the United States, public parks and the first forerunners of the garden city move-ment were in fact being developed as ways of making urban space more humanly habitable. A writer is not obliged to pro-vide a comprehensive picture of the world his work represents (despite the aspirations of such novelists as Balzac and Zola to do just that), and many writers are disposed to respond with special acuteness to what is most unsettling in the big picture. The mid-twentieth-century American critic R. P. Blackmur coined the phrase "techniques of trouble" to characterize this predisposition among the modernists. The late Dickens remains in full possession of his celebrated exuberance and his vivid sense of the amusing and the preposterous, but his metaphoric imagination of the city increasingly becomes a technique of trou-ble. There may well have been personal reasons why the aging Dickens should have taken a darker view of many things, in-cluding urban things, but all this means is that his own evolving emotional state predisposed him to pick up certain significant signals in the urban environment that he might otherwise have allowed to recede into the background. Through the radical originality of his metaphors he registers a profound perception that the mushrooming metropolis of the nineteenth century con-stitutes a fundamental, and worrisome, alteration of the nature of urban existence, that the growth of the city may be running out of control.

It is hard to know how much of this troubled vision was

picked up by contemporaneous writers and by those who came
after him. It is usually the comic-grotesque and satiric aspects
of Dickens that are thought of as his "influence" on other writers, but that may not be the whole story. Dostoevsky, as I have
already noted, was an attentive reader of his British contemporary, and the oppressively claustrophobic Petersburg setting
of *Crime and Punishment*, sweltering and reeking in the summer
heat, is as close to the pollution-laden, garbage-choked atmosphere of *Our Mutual Friend* as any novel of that age, though
the virtual contemporaneity of these particular novels (Dostoevsky's book appeared the year after Dickens's) suggests
imaginative affinity rather than borrowing. *Crime and Punishment* also incorporates apocalyptic perspectives, though these are
associated with industrialism, the mechanization of life and
thought, and rationalist revolutionary ideologies more than with
the city as such. It is instructive, however, that just as Eugene
Wrayburn has to undergo virtual death and rebirth in the countryside, Raskolnikov must come to the point of death and experience rebirth—in his case, an explicitly Christian rebirth—
in the empty expanses of Siberia, far from the teeming city.
Dickens, lacking Dostoevsky's imaginative anchorage in the
spiritual world of the Gospels, did not represent the city as a
modern equivalent of the New Testament realm of the wretched
that Jesus had come to redeem. For him, at least for fleeting but
powerful moments in his late novels, the city, under the impetus
of economic and technological modernity, seemed merely to be
turning into a dark arena of doom, without reference to scrip-
tural models. From our vantage point nearly a century and a
half later, with our own urban areas enveloped in layers of harm-
ful fumes, their arterial highways clogged, their inner cities ravaged by violence and crime, it may seem, at least at some moments, as though Dickens the visionary realist were seeing the
future in the London of his day.

The panoramic view of an excavation for Haussman's Parisian urban-
renewal project records the devastation wrought on the traditional city in order
to accomplish the new construction. Photograph by Charles Marville (1860s).
From Patrice Moncan and Claude Heurteux, *Le Paris de Haussman* (Paris:
Editions de Mécene, 2002).

This image of Paris in the rain in the 1880s, photographed by the novelist Emile Zola, captures something of the blurring of forms and the impeding of perception that Flaubert was drawn to in many of his urban scenes. From *La Parigi di Zola* (Rome: Editori Riuniti, 2001).

This image of the construction of an urban railway in London in the 1840s gives some sense of the violence done to the cityscape that Dickens represents in *Dombey and Son*. Photograph by Henry Flather (c. 1866). From *Photographer's London*, ed. Mike Seaborne (London: Museum of London, 1995).

A churchyard in London in Dickens's time, the shanty-like structures crowding out the light. Photograph by Alfred and John Bool (1877). From *Photographer's London*, ed. Mike Seaborne (London: Museum of London, 1995).

A forest of masts on the Thames, though not in flames, as they seem to be to the eye of the observer in *Our Mutual Friend*. Photograph by Morgan and Laing (c. 1876). From *Photographer's London*, ed. Mike Seaborne (London: Museum of London, 1995).

A photograph of a Thames scene in the 1860s shows the jumble of houses along the riverbank that makes itself felt in *Our Mutual Friend*. Photograph by James Hederly (c. 1870). From *Photographer's London*, ed. Mike Seaborne (London: Museum of London, 1995).

A working-class neighborhood along the Thames in Dickens's era, with an abundance of chimneypots on the roofs, is an intimation of the urban jumble Dickens represents in his novels. Photograph by William Strudwick (c. 1866). From *Photographer's London*, ed. Mike Seaborne (London: Museum of London, 1995).

A Thameside view in the 1860s, with St. Paul's, obscured by fog, in the
background. The business signs recall those that catch the eye of Eugene
and Mortimer as they glide down the river in *Our Mutual Friend.*
Photograph by Alfred Rosling (c. 1853). From *Photographer's London*, ed.
Mike Seaborne (London: Museum of London, 1995).

The London docks in the late nineteenth century. The looming proportions of
the ships are something registered by Dickens. Photographer unknown (1885).
From John Betjman, introduction and commentaries, *Victorian and Edwardian
London from Old Photographs* (New York: Viking, 1969).

These itinerant garbage collectors, begrimed and weary looking, suggest
the dehumanizing process of living off urban garbage that figures, from
the opening scene onward, in *Our Mutual Friend*. Photograph by John
Thompson (c. 1876). From Thompson, *Street Life in London* (1876; rpt. New
York: Benjamin Blom, 1969).

This view of London in the late nineteenth century, with images and contours
dissolving in the fog and the "cold disk" of the ineffectual sun above, recalls several fog scenes in *Our Mutual Friend*. Photograph by James Sinclair (c. 1913).
From *Photographer's London*, ed. Mike Seaborne (London: Museum of London,
1995).

The view of a grand public square in Petersburg, around the time of Bely's novel, catches the presence of fog even in broad daylight. Photographer unknown (c. 1910). From *Before the Revolution: St. Petersburg in Photographs*, ed. M. P. Iroshnikov (New York: Harry Abrams, 1991).

This Dublin street scene, taken roughly at the time *Ulysses* is set, illustrates the ubiquity of trams in the city. Photographer unknown (early 1900s). From Ian Gunn and Clive Hart with Harold Beck, *James Joyce's Dublin* (London: Thames and Hudson, 2004).

The house across the street from the house in which Kafka was born. Note the staring windows, reflecting the houses and the windows across the way. Photograph by Isidor Pollak. From Johann Bauer, *Kafka and Prague* (New York: Praeger, 1971).

5

Bely

Phantasmatic City

Ⅰf THE GREAT CAPITALS of
Western Europe become "new" cities during the nineteenth century because their exponential growth and the intervention of
modern technology transform the underlying nature of urban
experience, Petersburg is a new city in a stricter and more radical sense of the term. Created by an edict of Peter the Great
in 1703, it is the one European capital that is a through-and-
through planned city, an act of political will imposed on the
marshlands along the Neva River not far from the Finnish bor-
der by a tsar intent on westernizing and "rationalizing" his na-
tion. (Though the original name was St. Petersburg, or Saint
Peter's City, common Russian usage realistically identifies the
city with the tsar, not the saint, and calls it Petersburg, a practice followed by Andrei Bely in the title of his novel.) Instead
of the twisting ancient cowpaths turned into the lanes and
streets that mark so many old cities, Petersburg, like other
planned cities that followed it, was laid out on a rectilinear grid,
with spacious avenues, or prospects (Bely will make much of
this geometrical term), lined with stately town houses and grand
public buildings. The conception of the Italian architect Trez-

zini, whom Peter imported for the founding works, was to make this city, with its network of canals, a Venice of the North, a new kind of Russian capital wrenched from the cultural framework and the indigenous architectural traditions of medieval Russia.[1] As with more limited projects of urban planning elsewhere, the vision of a liberating rationalized order did not work itself out in neat accordance with the dreams of the planners. The marshland location made the city subject to dense fog that could often seem oppressive; the water supply, which quickly became polluted, rendered drinking anything that did not come out of a bottle a perilous act (then and now); and, most crucially, with the growth of population—more than a million and a half by the beginning of the twentieth century, 2,217,000 on the brink of World War I—wretched, crowded slums rapidly sprang up, as any reader of *Crime and Punishment* will vividly recall.

There are three writers from the period of the early twentieth century which is often now designated as the age of High Modernism who in strikingly innovative novels seek to convey the reality of a particular city as much as that of the actual characters: Virginia Woolf, imagining London in *Mrs. Dalloway;* Joyce, making Dublin, June 16, 1904, the dense medium for all that goes on in *Ulysses;* and Andrei Bely, who actually sets out the name of the city, *Petersburg,* as the title of the novel, almost as though the city, and not any of the individual characters (who are in any case rather less interesting than Joyce's or Woolf's), were his real subject. There is, let me say at the outset, a certain presumption in my undertaking to discuss this book, especially as part of a larger consideration of "the language of the novel," because I am unable to read it in the original. Its compelling relevance, however, to the general topic I am exploring makes me unwilling to forgo it, and because it is a novel that remains relatively unfamiliar to readers outside the orbit of Russian culture, there may be some virtue in the very act of drawing attention to its peculiar achievement. I feel less apprehensive than I might otherwise about dealing with *Petersburg* because I can draw on the scrupulous translation, finely attentive to linguistic detail, by Robert A. Maguire and John E. Malmstead, which also offers sixty pages of notes that illuminate many aspects of the Russian context as well as aspects of language that cannot be conveyed in translation.[2] In any case, I shall limit my comments on Bely's novelistic language to such features as imagery, motif, theme, and point of view that are more or less transparent in translation.

Bely's novel, like Woolf's and Joyce's, concentrates on a short span of time in the metropolis (in his case, nine days rather than the stretch of less than twenty-four hours of the two English-language novels), with the center of interest situated in the consciousness of the characters rather than in any unfolding of events that could constitute a real plot. Bely, however, breaks more sharply with the assumptions of the realist novel than Woolf or Joyce by repeatedly flaunting the status of his fiction as artifice. Some of the self-reflexive strategies he deploys hark back to such eighteenth-century practitioners of self-reflexive fiction as Fielding, Sterne, and Diderot: apostrophes to the reader, ironically descriptive chapter headings, sundry typographical shenanigans. But these insistent exposures of the fictionality of the fiction are impelled by a serious engagement in the philosophic issue of what constitutes reality, with the paradoxical consequence that self-reflexivity is turned into the instrument of a new kind of realism. Here, for example, are the narrator's reflections just before the end of the first chapter, as he is completing the initial movement of introducing us into his fictional world:

> In this chapter we have seen Senator Ableukhov. We have also seen the idle thoughts of the senator in the form of the senator's son, who also carries his own idle thoughts in his head. Finally, we have seen another idle shadow—the stranger.
>
> This shadow arose by chance in the consciousness of the Senator Ableukhov and acquired its ephemeral being there. But the consciousness of Apollon Apollonovich is a shadowy con-

sciousness because he too is the possessor of an ephemeral being and the fruit of the author's fantasy: unnecessary, idle cerebral play.

The author, having hung pictures of illusions all over, really should take them down as quickly as possible, breaking the thread of the narrative if only with this very sentence. But the author will not do so: he has sufficient right not to.

Cerebral play is only a mask. Under way beneath this mask is the invasion of the brain by forces unknown to us. And granting that Apollon Apollonovich is spun from our brain, nonetheless he will manage to inspire fear with another, a stupendous state of being which attacks in the night. Apollon Apollonovich is endowed with the attributes of this state of being.

Once his brain has playfully engendered the mysterious stranger, that stranger exists, really exists. He will not vanish from the Petersburg prospects as long as the senator with such thoughts exists, because thought exists too. (pp. 35–36)

The fact that the characters and images of the novel are projections of the writer's imagination—or if one prefers, distillations of his fantasies—proves to be not a special case peculiar to the condition of art but, on the contrary, an exemplary instance of how the mind relates to reality. We may well remain uncertain about the ontological grounding of the images that play across the screen of our minds, but it is only through the mind that we have access to everything that impinges upon us. The images on that inner screen, whether faithful replicas of things on the outside or biased, even fantastic, distortions, become our reality, just as the novelist's inventions, the "pictures of illusions" that he hangs all around, become a compelling reality, and one that refers to the real historical world (Petersburg, September 30 to October 9, on the brink of the revolution of 1905). In Bely's understanding, there is something at least potentially scary about these wavering mental images. As the novel unfolds it becomes clear that the scariness is generated both by impending political violence and by the nature of urban experience in Petersburg.

Two general aspects of this dynamic of self-reflexivity should be noted. Although Bely is hyperconscious of the fact that we are all captives of the mental pictures we make of the world, he does not mean to promote solipsism. We live incessantly with "cerebral play" (a phrase he invokes again and again in the course of the novel), but it "is only a mask," for the mind is constantly bombarded by real forces outside itself that it cannot really fathom. Second, Bely's very self-consciousness about the operations of the mind leads him technically not to a verbal simulation of the movement of consciousness, as in Joyce and Woolf, but rather to a narratorial overview, sometimes visually descriptive in character, of the workings of consciousness, a kind of hidden camera that pokes into the cranium—the cranial bone structure is much in evidence in the book—to follow, often in a manifestly visual fashion, the swirling progression of images and ideas going on in the brain.

All this, perhaps a little surprisingly, is intrinsically connected with the nature of the city that is the subject of the novel. One should observe that the figure of the mysterious stranger in this coda to the first chapter is set squarely in "the Petersburg prospects." Those prospects, in turn, are strongly associated from the opening pages of the novel with the spectral irreality of the city.

The prologue to the novel is a brief meditation not on the characters or the events that will follow but on the plan of the city, emphasizing the rectilinear and thoroughly European design of its principal avenue, Nevsky Prospect. Petersburg, unlike older cities, begins as an idea, which is then projected into three-dimensional space, and so there is a peculiar concordance between the actual nature of the city and its cartographic representation, and both of these in turn are linked with the artifice of fiction that conjures up the city:

> Petersburg not only appears to us, but actually does appear—
> on maps: in the form of two small circles, one set inside the
> other, with a black dot in the center; and from precisely this
> mathematical point, which has no dimension, it proclaims force-
> fully that it exists: from this very point surges and swarms the
> printed book. (p. 2)

A second concordance is observable in these lines, which set
the terms for much of what follows—between the emergence of
Petersburg as a real city from an abstract, quasi-mathematical
idea and the emergence of the multifaceted world of the novel
from the abstraction of typographical symbols on the printed
page. At this early point, Bely also introduces the term *swarm*—
the translators are careful throughout the book to render the
Russian *roi* consistently with this English equivalent—which
will be crucial to his representation of the phenomenology of
urban life. Bely had been a student of mathematics, and he makes
central to the elaborate structure of motifs (another characteristically modernist trait) two geometric figures that stand in
dialectic tension with each other, and on which is imposed the
third, antigeometric figure of the swarm. The rectilinear grid is
the figure for the planned capital city. It is also the defining
element of the mental life of Senator Ableukhov, the Petersburg
bureaucrat who dreams of squares, cubes, and grids projected to
infinity, who even rides in a cubelike carriage, and as government bureaucrat is thoroughly the creature of a mechanical rationality that seeks a sense of security in drawing endless
straight lines. Against the rectilinear grid stands the figure of
the sphere, which as Bely conceives it is inherently unstable,
threatening sudden and astronomic expansion. The sphere is
associated with the ticking bomb given by a revolutionary cell
to Ableukhov's son Nikolai with which to kill the old man. (The
parricide never happens. Like other attempts to execute portentous acts in the novel—with the partial exception of the murder
of one of the terrorists—high drama collapses into farce, and

all that the bomb destroys is a good deal of ceiling plaster.) The expanding sphere is also a figure of consciousness itself, with its powerful centrifugal impulse, its tendency to leap out to sidereal spaces and perhaps to run out of control. But if the sphere challenges the rectilinear stability of Petersburg on political grounds and in terms of the dynamics of the mind, the swarm threatens the planned city as an embodiment of the actual, uncontainable nature of the urban world. Here is a characteristic manifestation of swarm from the first chapter, appearing at the beginning of a section headed by the rubric *wet autumn*. It also vividly exemplifies Bely's febrile and distinctly unsettling manner of describing the city:

> Tufts of cloud scudded by in a greenish swarm. The greenish swarm rose ceaselessly over the interminable remoteness of the prospects of the Neva; into the greenish swarm stretched a spire ...from the Petersburg side.
>
> Describing a funereal arc in the sky, a dark ribbon, a ribbon of soot, rose from the chimneys; it tailed off into the waters.
>
> The Neva seethed and shrieked with the high-pitched whistle of a small steamboat, it smashed steely, watery shields against the piers of the bridges, and it lapped at the granite.
>
> And against this glooming background of hanging soot tailing above the damp stones of the embankment railing, eyes staring into the turbid germ-infested waters of the Neva, there stood, in sharp outline, the silhouette of Nikolai Apollonovich. (p. 29)

It is striking that this view of the city over the Neva has swarm above and swarm below—the ghoulishly greenish roiling mass of clouds over the city and the greenish miasma, presumably fog, rising from the Neva. Like Dickens, Bely is looking at a city enveloped in layers of pollution, "this glooming background of hanging soot," but he is less concerned with pollution as an ecological menace than as a medium that defines the field of human perception—here, as in a good many other places, the perception of the narrator rather than of a particular character. The greenish swarm of fog and cloud in effect negates the confident rectilinearity of the city. All that is clearly visible of Peter the Great's grand urban plan is the spire of Saints Peter and Paul Cathedral, thrusting up over the fortress to which it is attached (and in this respect rather like the dome of St. Paul's in *Our Mutual Friend*, last to go in the universal drowning). Those "turbid germ-infected waters of the Neva" are of course a threat to the human population living around them, yet what seems chiefly to concern Bely is not the issue of hygiene but rather the fact that the natural world, even in the heart of the city, harbors a pullulation of inchoate, alien life irresistibly asserting itself against the neat geometric design of the human planners. The river itself is not exactly personified, as Dickens perhaps might have done, but rather animated as a formless primordial beast, seething and shrieking and lapping at the granite foundations of the city. This vision of nature will have a correlation in Bely's vision of politics, which repeatedly figures the potentially revolutionary mob as a vast "myriopod."

What is most distinctive, however, about Bely's view of the city over the Neva is its manifestly fragmented character. The affinity with Flaubert is noteworthy, though there are important differences. The explicit literary allusions in the novel, mostly parodic, are predominantly to nineteenth-century Russian writers (Pushkin, Gogol, Dostoevsky, and Tolstoy), but it is a reasonable inference that Bely, like so many other Russian novelists, was also an attentive reader of Flaubert—including *The Sentimental Education*. Fragmentary perception in Bely differs because it is often not a mimetic representation of the limited and baffled observation of a particular character, though there are some spectacular instances in which this is the case. Bely, in keeping with his repeated gestures toward an eighteenth-century mode of self-reflexive fiction, by and large employs a narrator who makes himself quite ostentatiously the mediator between the reader and the represented world of the novel. In our passage, then, as often elsewhere in the book, the fragmented vision of the city is the narrator's. In one respect, this raises the stakes of fragmentation. When Frédéric Moreau in *The Sentimental Education* can take in only a whirl of fleeting images, we may be justified in regarding him as a sort of urban everyman, but the possibility exists that his disoriented vision is a function of his character as an unmoored soul in the city, a consciousness floating on the tides of desire, insulated in self-preoccupation, and thus ill-equipped to observe the reality around him with any clarity or balance. In Bely, the narrator's repeatedly fragmented vision of Petersburg suggests that there is something intrinsically resistant to comprehensive observation in the nature of the city. The fog that rolls up from the water is not merely a meteorological phenomenon but the emblematic manifestation of this urban reality. The eye of even a privileged observer, the narrator, can make out only dark ribbons of soot, the tip of a spire, a pair of staring eyes, in the midst of the greenish swarm; and elsewhere, when a crowd in the streets is described, it is seen as an amorphous creature with "myriad legs," "crawl[ing] sediment," part of "a black haze of phantasmata" (p. 179). Bely's Petersburg joins company with Dickens's London and Flaubert's Paris when the narrator comments early on that "Petersburg streets possess one indubitable quality: they transform passersby into shadows" (p. 22). The word *shadow* in fact is constantly reiterated—Maguire and Malmstead inform us that the Russian *ten'* has the semantic range of *shade, shadow,* and *ghost*—and Bely is endlessly resourceful in evoking qualities of flickering, treacherously phosphorescent light in the general murk:

> A shaft of light flew by: a black carriage flew by. Past window recesses it bore blood red lamps that seemed drenched in blood. They played and shimmered on the black waters of the Moika. The spectral outline of a footman's tricorne and the outline of the wings of his greatcoat flew, with the light, out of the fog and into the fog. (p. 33)

The half-invisible city is a threatening and perhaps nasty place. It is also, in Bely's treatment of it, as even this brief excerpt intimates, an elaborately aestheticized place: the red glimmering through the fog, a recurring color motif in the novel associated with revolutionary violence, plays against the ghastly green of the prevailing miasma; there are also repeated patches of yellow that are tied in with an Oriental motif (both a fashion of décor and a political menace in the Russia of 1905); and at a couple of points we get sunset scenes in which jewellike points of intense colored light burn across the darkening cityscape. But if Bely uses color to give aesthetic shape and thematic definition to his novel, what is fundamental to his sense of urban experi- ence is his constant insistence on disjunct images—in particular, body parts and bits of clothing—instead of coherent description. The staring eyes of Nikolai Ableukhov over the embankment railing—as far as the narrative lets us see, he has no body, only the eyes and (in the next paragraph) a leg shod in an overshoe— are exemplary of the way humanity is perceived in *Petersburg*. A few minutes later in narrative time than the passage with the eyes, Nikolai stands on an iron bridge: "And saw nothing. Above the damp railing, above the greenish waters teeming with germs, bowler, cane, coat, ears, nose, and mustache rushed by into the gusts of Neva wind" (p. 35). This narrative procedure, of course, is part of the suspense-generating mechanism of the detective novel that interests Bely as it does Dickens. (The suit- ability of the detective novel to the modern city is noteworthy: in the modern urban zone, there are menacing forces at work, lurking dangers, dark mysteries to be solved.) In 1905 Peters- burg there are many gentlemen with canes and bowlers walking through the streets, but the mustached figure in question, barely glimpsed by Nikolai as an assemblage of fragments, will have a sinister role to play in the book. This insistent displacement of whole figures by body fragments could well be an instance in which Bely pushes to an extreme a device of Tolstoy's (the as- sociation of characters with physical motifs, such as Karenin's protruding ears), as he does with other aspects of Tolstoy. The fragment here has an unsettling tendency to take over entirely, thus suggesting the impotence of vision itself.[3]

A fleeting, fragmentary image imperfectly seen readily becomes a trigger of anxiety, even paranoia, in the observer, who after all, would like to know what he is really looking at, what he has to confront. As such, it aptly serves the purposes of a tale of murky political conspiracy. But it is also the hallmark of perception in modern urban space, and Bely regularly links the fragmentary image with street scenes and crowds. Here is an exemplary instance. The unnamed "he" of the passage is again Nikolai:

> Amid the crowds that slowly flowed past, the stranger was flowing past. Or rather, he was flowing away in utter confusion from the intersection where he had been pressed against a carriage, from which stared an ear, a top hat.
>
> He had seen that ear before!
>
> He broke into a run.
>
> Cutting across columns of conversations, he caught fragments, and sentences took form.
>
> "Do you know?" was heard from somewhere on the right. And died away.
>
> And then surfaced:
>
> "They're planning . . ."
>
> "To throw . . ." (pp. 15–16)

There follows a page of this fragmentary dialogue, obviously pointing toward a plot to kill Ableukhov senior. The exchange of words heard through high interference is the perfect auditory equivalent of the broken field of visual perception that prevails throughout the novel: the eavesdropper, presumably Nikolai, is able to distinguish only shards of the conversation, and as they reach him, phrases get scrambled and ambiguities proliferate. Russian readers attest that Bely is an extraordinarily musical stylist, but it is clearly a music without melodic sequence. Au-

ditory as well as visual space is too crowded—there are multiple
"columns of conversations"—and everything around the observer is in flux. The ear that Nikolai suddenly recognizes is
actually his father's, the owner of a pair of ears protruding like
the handles of a jug several times satirically displayed in the
novel. This egregious ear sits under a top hat and not a bowler
because the more formal headpiece is part of the senator's attire
as a high-ranking bureaucrat. The perceptual alienation of the
observer from the observed, which lines up with Nikolai's emotional alienation from his father that is important in the plot, is
a striking instance of what happens to human relations in urban
reality: the young man is looking at the person with whom he
has the most intimate biological connection, yet at first he sees
not an integral image but perplexing fragments, an ear and a
top hat, and then the grotesque prominence of the ear leads him
to the correct, and troubling, identification.

Let me propose an interim summary of what constitutes a
distinctive language of the novel in Bely. The open license of
novelistic narration to invite a contemplation of its own fictive-
ness in the very act of compellingly deploying it makes possible
a double-edged ontological interrogation—of the status of the
fictional world and of the real world it purportedly represents.
In regard to the rendering of the city, the second of these two
interrogations has a decisive effect. Bely of course does not mean
to question whether there is a real Petersburg. His entire novelistic procedure, however, conveys a powerful sense that this is
a new kind of city that stands in a problematic relationship with
both human community and individual consciousness. The product of an abstract conception, it is not a place that has grown
organically through a long process of historical accretion,
though it does bear the marks of its relatively brief trajectory
through history, as Bely indicates in several significant passages.
As the preeminent Russian instance of the terrific density of
modern urban existence, it is shown as a theater of faceless
crowds in constant flux, where the isolate individual, shorn of

the comfort and assurance of the flâneur, makes his way, never entirely certain what is illusion and what is reality. In this connection, the freedom of novelistic report, strikingly inaugurated by Flaubert, to renounce the continuity of integral description in order to represent the discontinuous impingement of sensory stimuli on consciousness, plays a crucial role. What the observer, whether character or narrator, makes out in the fog-shrouded flux of this urban world is an ear, a pair of eyes, a mustache, a hat, and he is compelled to infer, or led to fear, what may lie behind these disjunct members. The fragmentary features glimpsed in the urban crowd might be parts of a face or of a mask, and so there is thematic appropriateness in the fact that a masked ball figures importantly in *Petersburg* as it does in *The Sentimental Education* (though Bely does not follow Flaubert in providing a kinetic evocation of the actual experience of the masked dance).

Phenomenologically, the traditional city is an extension of the house. The house, the basic structure of shelter and domestic life, has a roof to ward off rain, snow, and sun, walls to keep out the winds and the neighbors. Ideally, the city is a community of interconnected houses serving these purposes, with the sense of stable shelter enhanced by the walls that surround most ancient and medieval cities. Bely's Petersburg, like Flaubert's Paris, is represented as a place more of streets than of houses, and, even more notably, of opening and shutting doors. Everything here is imagined in transition—the family, history, politics, and, above all, consciousness itself. Here is the narrator commenting on Nikolai's experience of going through doorways:

> From time to time, while passing from the outer door to the inner door of the entryway, a certain strange, very strange state came over him, as if everything that was beyond the door was not what it was, but something else. Beyond the door there was nothing. If the door were to be flung open it would be flung open onto the measureless immensity of the cosmos, and the only thing left was to . . . plunge into it headfirst and fly past

stars and planetary spheres, in an atmosphere of two hundred and seventy-three degrees below zero. (p. 164)

This sort of sudden lurch of consciousness over a threshold into sidereal space, or into an abyss, is a distinctively modernist move (though there are, as we saw, some episodic intimations of such an explosion of perspective in Dickens's metaphors). One might recall the leap outward from Leopold Bloom's thoughts and conversation to the infinity of the starry expanses—and in fact to the absolute zero of outer space, the temperature at which motion is no longer possible—in the great Ithaca section of *Ulysses*. Much of the dynamic of *Petersburg* is implicated in the experience registered here of wrenching and unpredictable transition. Thus, at the beginning of the sixth chapter, we are given a brief but significant notation of how Doodkin, the apocalyptic revolutionary, feels upon waking up in the morning: "The transitional state between wakefulness and sleep was as if he were jumping out of a narrow window from the fourth floor. Sensations were opening a breach: he was flying into this breach" (p. 169). Later, the novel offers its most spectacular rendering of a transitional state of consciousness in Lippanchenko's transition from life to death as he is stabbed in the back. With Bely's anthroposophic beliefs in the background, this is oddly but interestingly represented as an expansion of consciousness: "The monstrous periphery of consciousness sucked the planets into itself, and sensed them as organs detached from one another. The sun swam in the dilations of the heart, and the spine grew incandescent from the touch of Saturn's masses: a volcano opened up in his stomach" (pp. 263–264).

Several different ideas are entangled in this preoccupation with states of violent transition. Bely sees consciousness as inherently volatile, subject to disruptive dilation or contraction, like the image of the explosive sphere to which he reverts. History equally participates in this volatility, as the setting of the novel after the debacle of the Russo-Japanese War and on the eve of the revolution of 1905 is intended to remind us. Finally, situating the novel in the modern capital city evokes a collective space that both embodies and fosters transitionality. Petersburg is seen as a politically willed disruption of the traditional course of Russian history. As a breeding ground of transition—including the violent political transition of revolution—it produces a "swarm" of individuals isolated from one another in whom any sense of confident stability is subverted by the kinetic discontinuities of urban experience. The swirling, obfuscating insubstantiality of the fog becomes the sickly green mirror of the texture of their lives.

Petersburg is an acutely visual novel, and so its pervading sense of sudden disruption in the modern city is repeatedly translated into arresting visual imagery. This metropolis of 1905 is the first of the cities we are considering that is lit by electric lights, and Bely at several points calls attention to the sheer on-and-off abruptness of electric lighting, in contrast to the relative gradualness of its gaslit predecessor. Thus Lieutenant Likhutin, the husband who fears he has been cuckolded by Nikolai and who will make a farcical attempt at suicide, paces about his apartment vigorously turning off the lights and wondering whether there may be some peculiar link between the lights and his marital woes:

> What in the world was the connection between all *this disgusting business* and the electric lights? There was just as little sense in it as in the connection between the angular, sad figure of the second lieutenant in a dark green uniform, and the goatee provocatively adorning a face that seemed carved from fragrant wood. There was no connection at all. Except in the mirror. . . .
> "Click" went the switches, plunging the man and his gestures into darkness. Perhaps this was not Second Lieutenant Likhutin? (pp. 131–132)

A mirror—Bely is as fond of them as his admirer Nabokov will be—offers an image of the self that can be perceived as alien to the self. The sudden plunge into darkness through the flick of the light switch is a violent disruption of the visual field, a subversion of confidence in the persistence of the figure that stands in the visual field. Bely's novelistic procedure thus opens questions, as Proust, at about the same time, was doing in a more ruminative fashion, about the very continuity of the self. There is no causal connection between turning off the lights and cuckoldry, though perhaps it may make the second lieutenant think subliminally of the adulterous "deed of darkness," but it does intimate something like an abrupt break in identity: the dignified army officer in his dark green uniform has been reduced, at least so he fears, by his wife and her lover to a pathetic figure of fun, or to nothing at all, swallowed up in darkness.

Bely's deployment of sudden and uncertain illumination and its extinguishing ranges from a kind of anxious comedy, as in the instance of Likhutin, to sinister suspense. Here is Doodkin, the would-be revolutionary, in a cinematic, and, indeed, Hitchcockian, moment lighting a match on the staircase of his boardinghouse. (One might recall that Walter Benjamin, discussing modern urban experience in his essay on Baudelaire, mentions the invention of the match as something that contributed to the shaping of a new mode of staccato perception.) At the point in time of the early 1920s when Bely was completing the revision of his novel, he would have in all likelihood been exposed to some compelling instances of silent film, both Russian and German, but there is no way of knowing whether he was actually influenced by cinematic technique or, rather, intuitively anticipating it.

> Throwing down a lighted match, he leaned over the banister and cast a frightened glance. The balasters of the banister flared up. In the flickering light he could clearly discern silhouettes.
>   One proved to be that Makhmoud fellow, the denizen of the basement. In the light cast by the falling match Makhmoud was

whispering to an ordinary looking little fellow, who was wearing the expected bowler: he had an Oriental face with a hook
nose.

   The match went out. (p. 202)

The match combines the suddenness of the electric light
with the flickering quality of the candle and manifestly height-
ens the occluded perception of fleeting fragments to which this
novel is so attached. If a light turned off or gone out is a sudden
disruption of visual experience, Bely also sometimes represents
illumination itself, whether electric glare, stroboscopic flash, or
wavering candlelight, as a violent act. Most strikingly, and also
most appositely, we are invited to see in the following terms the
candle Lippanchenko carries up to his bedroom moments before
he will be murdered: "The candle cut into the room. The pitch
blackness was torn apart. Fragments of darkness whirled about
the periphery of a flaming, dancing center; and beyond the dark
wedges which were the shadows cast by objects was a shadow,
an enormous dark fat man" (p. 261). The huge fat man is Lippanchenko himself, his shadow having turned into an image of
the self alienated from the self and perceived as other, like the
goateed face in the mirror of the second lieutenant.

   This pervasive apprehension of sudden rupture is projected
onto the plane of history in the broodings about apocalypse to
which considerable space is devoted. The apocalyptic imaginings
are quite different from the ones we looked at in Dickens, not
only because the Dickensian apocalypse is no more than a fleeting glimpse contained in a comic framework but also because
Bely's apocalypse is tied up with politics and the fate of cultures
rather than with the fate of the environment. Russia's defeat at
the hands of a rising Asian power and the imminence of violent
revolution lead the narrating consciousness and several of the
characters to fears that all of European civilization is about to
be engulfed in cataclysmic destruction. Here is the narrator's

report of Nikolai meditating on the dread bomb with which he has been entrusted: "Everything, everything, everything: this sunlit glitter, the walls, the body, the soul—everything would crash into ruins. Everything was already collapsing, collapsing, and there would be: delirium, abyss, bomb" (p. 157). Earlier in the book, the narrator, in a Pushkin-inspired apostrophe that conjures up the Bronze Horseman come to life and galloping across Russia, invokes the tones of the Book of Revelation: "There will be a leap across history. Great shall be the turmoil. The earth shall be cleft. The very mountains shall be thrown down by the cataclysmic earthquake.... Earth-born creatures once more will sink to the depths of the oceans, into chaos, primordial and long-forgotten" (p. 65).

Bely's apocalyptic view of history is powerfully imagined but not, I think, altogether coherent, and he seems to vacillate in what he wants to say on this score. The slightly odd concluding paragraphs of the novel in any case provide some perspective on the widening circles of cultural implication spreading out from the cartographic dot that is the modern European city Petersburg. The plot of parricide has collapsed; Nikolai's estranged parents have been reconciled, after a fashion; Ableukhov senior is retired from government service and reduced to doddering infirmity—while Nikolai travels through the Orient, staying for two years in Egypt, where he devotes himself to amateur scholarship. We get a glimpse of him contemplating the Sphinx (the Sophoclean version of the sphinx, of course, is associated with Oedipus, whose fate Nikolai came close to repeating). Egypt and the Sphinx stand at the hazy origins of our culture, but they are also alien to the tradition of rationalism that evolved in the West. In this Near Eastern context, Kant—the novel's exemplar of European rational thought—"is forgotten." Nikolai's native city is for the novelist the supreme instance of an attempt to impose rational order through an act of will on the recalcitrant stuff of history. In Bely's somber view, which is a strong instance of the darker side of modernism, this overweening urban project cannot hold together. It is an attempt to contain forces of disruption that resist containment. It is the collective implementation of a European faith in reason that has played itself out. The peculiar concluding note of *Petersburg* expresses in the same breath a sense of cultural exhaustion and an anticipation of universal destruction, and as such it participates in an apocalyptic meditation on the fate of European culture common to a number of prominent modernist works. Nikolai, brooding over the crumbling monumental sculpture of the Egyptian Sphinx, is led to reflect: "Culture is a moldering head: everything in it has died: nothing has remained. There will be an explosion: everything will be swept away" (p. 292). These are, of course, the gloomy thoughts of a defeated character, left after his aborted revolutionism without purposeful direction, aimlessly voyaging as Frédéric Moreau does at the end of *The Sentimental Education*. The city is the image of his defeat, the wavering apparition of sinister illusions and ominous prospects of destruction. The novel that began with Nevsky Prospect and the rectilinear plan of the city ends with a retreat to the countryside: Nikolai, having returned to Russia after the deaths of his parents, retires to their rural estate, marching about the woods in "gloomy indolence," having put Petersburg and the Promethean enterprise in history it embodies forever behind him.

Both the pervading apprehension of impending historical catastrophe and the sense of cultural exhaustion are markers of Bely's modernist moment, or at any rate, of the prominent downside of modernism that his novel vividly reflects. But what *Petersburg* also abundantly calls to our attention is a certain correlation between the modern city as a construct of human design and technology and the modern novel as an inventive assemblage of self-conscious, sometimes iconoclastic, artifices. This means that together with the gloom and the historical pessimism, this novel often exhibits an exuberance, at least in its play with technique, which is a distant cousin, less openly celebratory, to the exuberance about modern urban reality in the paintings of Léger, Mondrian, and some of the Italian Futurists, to the poetry of Hart Crane, and to much else in the modernist movement. Bely sees the city as spectral, menacing, disorienting, but also as a privileged arena of "cerebral play," with the imaginative pleasures attendant on it. At roughly the same time, many hundreds of miles to the west, Virginia Woolf and James Joyce were exploring tonally and technically different but related possibilities of representing the modern city in novelistic space as a playground for the imagination.

6

Woolf

Urban Pastoral

To JUDGE BY THE NOVELS we
have considered so far, the modern metropolis seems to earn a
triple-A rating for angst, alienation, and anomie, with a certain
appropriateness in the trilingualism of the alliterative triplet if
one thinks of the pan-European scope of these urban patholo-
gies. This somber view of the city is not merely the reflection
of the writers' private obsessions (although of course it is often
also that), for there is abundant evidence that the unprecedented
demographic mushrooming within urban space throughout the
nineteenth century and on into the twentieth was rarely
matched by a collective ability to order that space effectively
and make it attractively habitable for individuals and commu-
nities. Our continuing problems in the twenty-first century with
urban crime, crowding and squalor, traffic, and pollution suggest
that we are still far from finding our way out of this historical
impasse.

Yet most people who live in great cities, including the three
cities we have looked at up till now through a novelistic prism,
are likely to conclude that these dire visions represent a rather
partial view. The vast new cities are also places of excitement

and enlivening energy that can elicit a sense of exuberance in the urbanite. This upbeat sense of the city may be enhanced by grand avenues and gracious parks and other manifestations of enlightened urban planning, but it is chiefly the consequence of the sheer teeming variety of city life, superabundant in varying human types, fashions, merchandise, vehicles, architecture, and cultural activity. Just as in painting there is a modernism that responds enthusiastically to the exciting rhythms of modern urban existence—Léger and Mondrian do this in radically different ways—there is a current in modernist writing that registers a sense of affirmation quite unlike the themes of anguish and apocalypse which criticism so often associates with modernism. This affirmative trend in modernism has been finely described in *The Art of Celebration* by Alfred Appel Jr., a critic whose evocative prose emulates the celebratory mood of the writers, painters, sculptors, composers, and jazz musicians he admires.[1] Appel does not devote particular attention to Virginia Woolf, but her representation of London in *Mrs. Dalloway* is a vivid literary instance of the modernist art of celebration.

To make this claim in no way implies that Woolf should be seen as a cheerfully optimistic writer. She famously had her demons, and they are much in evidence in *Mrs. Dalloway*. Their main locus here, of course, is the figure of Septimus Warren Smith, who serves as an alter ego not only for Clarissa Dalloway, viscerally identifying as she does with his suicide when she hears of it at her party, but also for Woolf herself. The novelist's bouts of severe depression, accompanied by excruciating hypersensitivity and suicidal impulses, are transferred to this young veteran of the Great War and given a historical grounding in his traumatic battlefield experience.

If the war has inflicted unspeakable wounds, London five years after the end of hostilities is also seen in the book as a place of renewal. Peter Walsh, just having returned to London on this sunny June day of 1923 after five years in India, notices that "people looked different."[2] Change is in the air, manifested in an insouciant flouting of old conventions in public behavior, dress, the things people write about. Clarissa Dalloway, not having gone anywhere (except, one might say, to the brink of death in her illness during the great flu epidemic of 1919), is less interested in change than in memory. The novel in fact begins, after the brief notation that Clarissa is off to buy flowers and is making other preparations for her party, with a memory that flashes back from 1923 to the late 1880s, when Clarissa was an eighteen-year-old at the country house in Bourton, standing by the open French windows and on the verge of the dangers and excitements of life unfolding. This interweaving of present and past, town and country, creates at the outset the enabling framework for a mode of imagination that I shall call, with a backward glance at a well-known eighteenth-century poetic genre, urban pastoral. What that means above all for Woolf is that urban experience, seen quite vividly in its abundant particularities, can provide the sense of invigoration, harmony with one's surroundings, and enrapturing aesthetic revelation that is traditionally associated with the green world of pastoral. Clarissa remembers herself poised at the French windows seeing flowers and trees and smoke winding through the air and rooks rising and falling in a wavelike rhythm that she will repeatedly feel in London on this June day. In a kind of cinematic *faux raccord*, she is now revealed perched on the edge of the curb ready to cross the street, as she once stood poised at the open windows.

Like Bely's *Petersburg*, this is a novel much concerned with crossing thresholds. In Bely, however, the experience of transition, as we observed, is wrenchingly disorienting, even terrifying. In Woolf, what lies beyond the threshold may also be scary—the eighteen-year-old Clarissa feels "that something awful was about to happen" (p. 3), and much later in the book Septimus will actually plunge from the window all the way to his death. But taking the leap in this novel—perhaps even for Septimus—is also imagined as an opportunity, a plunge into the

intoxicating fullness of life. Thus the first proper picture of London we get, with Clarissa evidently still perched on the curb
and Big Ben ringing the hour, is an unabashed celebration of
the surge of activity in the street and all around:

> For Heaven only knows why one loves it so, how one sees it
> so, making it up, building it round one, tumbling it, creating it
> every moment afresh; but the veriest frumps, the most dejected
> of miseries sitting on doorsteps (drink their downfall) do the
> same; can't be dealt with, she felt positive, by Acts of Parliament
> for that reason: they love life. In people's eyes, in the swing,
> tramp, and trudge; in the bellow and the uproar; the carriages,
> motor cars, omnibuses, vans, sandwich men shuffling and
> swinging; brass bands; barrel organs; in the triumph and the
> jingle and the strange high singing of some aeroplane overhead
> was what she loved; life; London; this moment of June. (p. 4)

It is hard to think of another novel in which the simplest
deictic terms—*this, there, now*—are made to carry such thematic
significance. "This moment in June" here at the beginning points
the way through the book to the famous last sentence, which is
Peter's suddenly excited perception of Clarissa in the midst of
the party revealed in her full individual being: "For there she
was" (p. 194). London, entrancing the beholder as a constant
kinetic revelation of presences, is a pulsating tide—elsewhere,
the wave image is an explicit metaphorical comparison, but here
it is merely implied by the sheer rhythm of the prose "in the
swing, tramp, and trudge; in the bellow and the uproar." But it
is worth noting that there is a crucial difference in this book in
the interaction between consciousness and the urban scene from
what one encounters in Flaubert and Bely. Although Bely has
some notion of the mind's somehow shaping its own contents
through what he calls "cerebral play," he shares with Flaubert a
sense that the city showers consciousness with an overabundance of fleeting stimuli that induce a certain disorientation, that transform observation into phantasmagoria or hallu-

cination, and his notion of cerebral play does not seem to involve much purposeful poetic construction. In *Mrs. Dalloway*, that condition of mental confusion pertains only to Septimus, who is, after all, deranged. The two dominant centers of consciousness in the novel, Clarissa and Peter, both have an awareness of the mind's constructing the world around it from the materials that the world gives it, "making it up, building it round one, tumbling it, creating it every moment afresh." In *The Sentimental Education*, consciousness is in most respects acted upon by an elusive and multifarious urban reality constantly in motion. In *Mrs. Dalloway*, consciousness puts all these things together. This is the very rationale for Woolf's technique of lyric interior monologue. It also explains why the principal characters feel not estranged or confounded by the urban setting but, on the contrary, exhilarated by it. This early passage exhibits one small manifestation of the mind's integrative work on the sensory data given it when the buzzing of the plane overhead is represented as a "strange high singing," which by this choice of language is orchestrated with the music of the brass bands and the barrel organs. The urban scene bestows on consciousness a plethora of materials, and consciousness, through the very act of building it all into patterns, feels enriched, not daunted, by what it receives.

Urban crowds and urban dwellings, as we saw in Flaubert and Bely, may reinforce a sense of isolation in individuals which, pushed to the extreme, becomes an incipient solipsism or paranoia. This feeling of being cut off from meaningful human connections finds a congenial medium in modes of narration—pioneered by Flaubert—that are rigorously centered in the consciousness of the character. What is especially interesting about the representation of urban experience in *Mrs. Dalloway* is the sense conveyed of a dialectic interplay between isolation and connection. An engaging case in point is Peter Walsh's fanciful pursuit of the pretty young woman with the red carnation whom he encounters walking through Trafalgar Square. He is pleased to imagine himself a buccaneer on the high seas on the

track of fleeing treasure, and one wonders whether this harmless
exercise in voyeurism may have been inspired by Bloom's frustrated mental pursuit of the girl in the brown silk stockings in
the Lotus-eaters episode of *Ulysses*, published chapters of which
Woolf had been reading around the time she was beginning to
work on *Mrs. Dalloway*. When the young woman finally disap-
pears into a house, Peter recognizes, wryly but not altogether
regretfully, that "it was smashed to atoms—his fun, for it was
half made up, as he knew very well; invented, this escapade with
the girl; made up, as one makes up the better part of life, he
thought—making oneself up; making her up; creating an exquisite amusement, and something more" (p. 54). What strikes
him as odd and perhaps a little sad about this interior theater
stage-managed by the imagination, with which one lives more
or less constantly, is that "all this one could never share." The
interior monologues of *Mrs. Dalloway* repeatedly carry us into
private realms built with metaphors and personal associations
that cannot be shared, yet the novel also abounds in moments
of sharing, which culminate in Clarissa's weird experience of
somehow sharing, through an imaginative leap, Septimus's suicide. London is not just a screen for projections but a space in
which interinvolved lives play themselves out and in which collective experience, present and past, is keenly felt. A moment
after the vanishing of the girl with the red carnation, Peter
reflects on the scene before him and on the reality of London it
conveys:

> It was a splendid morning too. Like the pulse of a perfect heart,
> life struck straight through the streets. There was no fum-
> bling—no hesitation. Sweeping and swerving, accurately, punc-
> tually, noiselessly, there precisely at the right moment, the
> motor-car stopped at the door. The girl, silk-stockinged,
> feathered, evanescent, but not to him particularly attractive (for
> he had had his fling), alighted. Admirable butlers, tawny chow
> dogs, halls laid in black and white lozenges with white blinds
> blowing, Peter saw through the opened door and approved of.

A splendid achievement in its own way, after all, London; the
season; civilisation. (pp. 54–55)

The inner theater has moved out-of-doors. Peter has shifted
from fantasist and voyeur to celebratory flâneur. (Though I began by proclaiming the demise of the flâneur, Peter remains a
rather vivid instance of the type.) What he celebrates in this
particular instance is the choreographed rituals of culture, or as
he puts it, "civilisation," which offers the observer this spectacle
of upper-class life, with its motorcars and fashionably dressed
young women, its marble-floored residences presided over by
dignified butlers. The great city is a place for the spectacular
display of *grand luxe* as well as of wretchedness, and though the
novel does look into the wretchedness at a few points, it is patently more at home imaginatively with the propertied classes,
whose elegant social ceremonies sometimes intimate the possibility of a gracious shared life. (It is worth noting that this novel
embraces a rather limited area of the geographical expanse of
London, most of it easily traversed by foot.) That arresting simile which occurs to Peter, "the pulse of a perfect heart," perfectly
expresses his perception of vital interconnection as he looks at
the busy city streets. The book that began with a view of the
outside through open French windows here gives us a perspective from the outside in through a door briefly opened. Later,
when Peter is walking from his hotel to the Dalloways' for the
party, he will see a whole series of doors opening as people
depart for their evening activities. An open door or window is
not a mirror or a screen but an aperture through which you can
actually see something of interest. The city is, among other
things, a great spectacle, perceived as such with special keenness
by Peter, who has just returned from five years in the colonial
provinces.

Clarissa exhibits an equally keen enjoyment of the spectacle—it is her deepest affinity with Peter—though in her case
the enjoyment is sharpened not by the contrast of expatriation

but by her recent brush with death, for, like Peter, she associates London with life. The interiorization of narration decisively inaugurated by Flaubert and later developed in a variety of related techniques placed in the foreground of the represented world of the novel the immediate sensory experience of the character. What Woolf does in *Mrs. Dalloway*, perhaps more than in any of her other books, and what Joyce does in a roughly analogous way in *Ulysses*, is to construct a system of values based on the vital presence of immediate sensory impressions. There is a link between her repeated reflections on mortality and the sheer presentness of London on this June day, its bright intensity offering a kind of rejoinder to the dark thoughts on death:

> What she loved was this, here, now, in front of her; the fat lady in the cab. Did it matter then, she asked herself, walking towards Bond Street, did it matter that she must inevitably cease completely; all this must go on without her; did she resent it; or did it not become consoling to believe that death ended absolutely? but that somehow in the streets of London, on the ebb and flow of things, here, there, she survived, Peter survived, lived in each other, she was positive, of the trees at home; of the house there, ugly, rambling all to bits and pieces as it was; part of people she had never met. (p. 9)

Narration consistently enacted through the point of view of the character easily conveys a feeling of the character's being imprisoned within the limits of his or her field of perception. Bely's repeated, rather unsettling representation of the cranial bones within which mental activity takes place offers a vivid anatomical image for the sense of being boxed in by the privateness of consciousness. For Clarissa the pulsating presence of the world—"this, here, now, in front of her"—has the power to break through the barriers of the private consciousness that constantly registers and constructs the world. The undulating life-rhythm of the city (a counterpart to Peter's pulse of the urban heart) carries her, still alive, beyond the prospect of her own inevitable death as well as beyond the prison of her own subjectivity. And so she entertains the idea, straddling fantasy and existential revelation, of being part of everything around her, even "part of people she had never met" (which will prove to be the climactic case when she learns of Septimus's death). In the clause immediately after the point where our excerpt breaks off, she will imagine herself "laid out like a mist, . . . spread ever so far," the very antithesis of Bely's image of the enclosed box of the cranium. This fantasy of interfusion then leads her to recall with a certain note of acceptance the song from *Cymbeline* about the transience of life, a text to which she will revert several times later. The diction of her own interior monologue at this point momentarily becomes vaguely Shake-spearian as she affirms human persistence in the face of loss: "This late age of the world's experience had bred in them all, all men and women, a well of tears. Tears and sorrows; courage and endurance; a perfectly right and stoical bearing" (pp. 9–10).

Fragmentation, as we have seen, is an essential element in the experience of the modern metropolis as an incessant shower of heterogeneous and largely unconnected stimuli rain down on the senses. What Woolf tries to do in *Mrs. Dalloway* is imagine a kind of unity in the heterogeneity or at least a sort of unity imposed by the perceiving consciousness that enables it to exult in the heterogeneity instead of being disoriented by it. Here is Peter, setting off from his hotel for Clarissa's, with the convic-tion that he is about to have "an experience," though he is un-certain what it will be:

> Beauty anyhow. Not the crude beauty of the eye. It was not beauty pure and simple—Bedford Place leading into Russell Square. It was straightness and emptiness of course; the sym-metry of a corridor; but it was also windows lit up, a piano, a gramophone sounding; a sense of pleasure-making hidden, but now and again emerging when, through the uncurtained win-dow left open, one saw parties sitting over tables, young people slowly circling, conversations between men and women, maids

idly looking out (a strange comment theirs, when work was done), stockings drying on top ledges, a parrot, a few plants. Absorbing, mysterious, of infinite richness, this life. (p. 163)

Peter's and Clarissa's perceptions of the London streets are antithetically complementary. She, wife, mother, and society hostess, experiences in her most intense apprehensions of the urban scene a quasi-physical merging of self and scene. He, the aging bachelor (once briefly married), colonial functionary, a man who has never quite found his niche in the world, observes the scene with a similar celebratory feeling, but from a certain distance, on the street, as spectator. As before he glanced into a house through an opened door, here he peers up at lit windows, taking in what he can through eye and ear in a way that is faintly tinged with voyeurism (the "sense of pleasure-making hidden" is vague enough but in its idiomatic form delicately hints at the possible inclusion of something sexual in the phrase). The sundry discrete items that impress themselves on Peter's senses do not make an intrinsic unity, but he assembles a kind of unity out of them in construing them all as disparate manifestations of life with its impulse of daily and seasonal and generational renewal—a few lines further on, he is moved by a glimpse of young couples, "dallying, embracing, shrunk up under the shower of a tree." All these oddly matched scraps of observation, as expressions of "this life," become for him "not beauty pure and simple" but a kind of sustaining beauty nevertheless.

Two kinds of relation of self to the urban setting, one rather more difficult than the other, are explored in *Mrs. Dalloway.* The first, which we have just been observing in operation, is the relation of peripatetic spectator to the bustling panoramic scene, and this is shared to some degree by Peter and Clarissa. The second, which is Clarissa's particular preoccupation, is the relation of the self to all those unknown others who so densely populate the city. A large city, as this novel often reminds us, is a place where one catches glimpses of faces rapidly passing or about to be hidden behind shades pulled down, and one can only guess what might be the lives behind those fleeting images. Near the beginning of the novel, Woolf offers a public instance of this experience of blocked visual access and frustrated knowledge in the backfiring government limousine that pulls up across the street from the florist's shop in which Clarissa is standing. A face is seen for a moment against dove-gray upholstery, then a male hand draws a blind, and the identity of the hidden figure in the car becomes an object of speculation for everyone in the vicinity. The more elaborate instance of occluded vision and knowledge is the old lady in the window of the house opposite, who first appears about halfway into the novel and then, with added thematic weight, just before the end. Clarissa's eye catches the old lady, about whom she knows almost nothing, moving away from the window to the back of her bedroom from where her white cap can still be made out. This, Clarissa reflects, is "the supreme mystery" for which neither religion nor reason nor even love had any real solution, and it "was simply this: here was one room; there another" (p. 127). In the evening while the party is going on, Clarissa has another brief sighting of the old woman pulling the blind, and then turning out the light as she prepares to go to bed. This image triggers in her mind still another recollection of "Fear no more the heat of the sun," the meditation on mortality from the song in *Cymbeline*, followed by an oddly happy thought about the courage of Septimus in throwing his life away, and then a resolution to return to the party with the recognition that "she must assemble" (p. 186).

The existential reflection inscribed in this concatenation of ideas is not unique to life in the city, but urban existence fosters it in a particular way. The city is a place of many windows facing other windows, in which human figures are imperfectly seen, and also look out. Kafka, as we shall see, with the power of paranoid vision that pervades *The Trial*, emphasizes the being looked at rather than seeing: unknown neighbors peering down from windows see Joseph K. being made into a spectacle at the beginning, and there may be someone at a window witnessing his execution at the end. Woolf concentrates on the seeing because her protagonist is attempting to reach out to the supreme mystery of "here . . . one room; there another." Clarissa cannot really bridge the chasm of separation: each of us is inescapably confined in the prison of our subjectivity (the metaphor of the prison is actually invoked a few pages later as Clarissa speaks with her girlhood friend Sally Seton), and the city, with its myriad windows where blinds go down and lights go out, is the palpable embodiment of that existential confinement. What, then, is the associative logic of Clarissa's thoughts at this fraught moment as the novel moves toward a resolution? Big Ben rings out again as the old lady lowers the blind, reminding Clarissa of the inexorable movement of time. The light goes out in the window across the way, and this darkness preparatory to sleep makes her think of death—almost simultaneously, of the song from *Cymbeline* and Septimus's suicide. Death, perhaps especially when it is freely embraced, sharpens the contrasting sense of being alive: "He made her feel the beauty; made her feel the fun." Clarissa, locked within the confines of her consciousness as each of us is, can achieve a liberation of sorts through two different acts, the one imaginative and the other social. At least for a moment, she understands Septimus from within (as she does not understand the old lady) because the bold extremeness of his decision to end his life speaks to her sense of the fragile beauty of being alive in the face of the grim inevitability of dying. The shared fate of mortality, grasped in a flash of imagination, becomes a bridge between the separate rooms. But Woolf recognizes, in the associative chain she provides her protagonist, that this sort of identification with another—another whom Clarissa has never actually seen—is both a revelation and a nonevent, a moment, after all, of significant fantasy and nothing more. Clarissa, of course, lives in her consciousness but equally in the social world, and thus she realizes that it is time for her to go back to the party, where she "must assemble"—a slightly ambiguous verb in context that may refer to pulling herself together and at the same time to pulling people together at the party, which is her vocation as hostess. The great modern city, as we have been observing in all these novels, is not a place of community. Its diffusion of social structures and its very architecture heighten the sense of "here . . . one room; there another." But a party is, at best, an attempt to constitute a small and temporary community—necessarily superficial in most respects, but not entirely so, as the revelation of Clarissa's vital presence to Peter at the very end is meant to intimate. It is to this possibility of creating connection in the social realm that Clarissa descends from her vantage point at the window in the room upstairs. Her party, where moments of community might be realized, is the exact antithesis of the orgiastic ball in Flaubert, where real identities are literally masked and the observing consciousness is trapped in a whirl of images suffused with the projective energies of its own desires.

A city seen through the consciousness of a character is necessarily seen in the narrative present (the predominant case in Flaubert), or in the present interwoven with fragments of the personal past of the character (often the case for Clarissa, as it is for both Stephen and Bloom in *Ulysses*). Yet a city presents itself to the awareness of the observer not only as a densely various set of sensory data in the present moment but also as a kind of archeological site, showing traces of its passage through a series of historical strata. The centering of narration in consciousness in fact facilitates this archeological perception of the city because consciousness, though constantly impinged upon by present stimuli, can also exert great freedom in reverting to the cultural past. Bely, as I briefly noted, does introduce a number of passages that register the trajectory of Petersburg through historical time, though all of these are discursive reflections by the narrator. Woolf, restricting her narration much more rigorously to the consciousness of the characters, motivates these

long temporal perspectives through the preoccupations and the
cultural experience of the characters. In fact, one of the most
deeply interesting aspects of the representation of the city in
Mrs. Dalloway is a dialectic interplay between London, palpably
seen and felt on this June day of 1923, with all its visible post-
war fashions and social mores, and the millennial city that goes
all the way back to the Romans. Rezia, Septimus's wife, on her
first appearance in the novel, feeling foreign and isolated in the
British metropolis, appropriately thinks as an Italian of the distant moment when the Romans first encountered this place:
"perhaps at midnight, when all boundaries are lost, the country
reverts to its ancient shape, as the Romans saw it, lying cloudy,
when they landed, and the hills had no names and rivers wound
they knew not where" (p. 24). Rezia's mental picture of the Ro-
man landing on the shore of the Thames is a reflection of her
own sense of estrangement from her present surroundings, but
it also serves to introduce a long perspective that plays a more
thematically central role elsewhere in the novel. The capacity
to project backward through millennia is complemented by a
projection to the future through millennia, and thus this bustling twentieth-century city is tied in with the broodings about
transience that Clarissa in particular harbors in relation to her
own life. When she sees the motorcar with its unidentified au-
gust passenger, she imagines him as

> the enduring symbol of the state which will be known to cu-
> rious antiquaries sifting the ruins of time, when London is a
> grass-grown path and all those hurrying along the pavement
> this Wednesday morning are but bones with a few wedding
> rings mixed up in their dust and the gold stoppings of innu-
> merable decayed teeth. (p. 16)

Woolf's most eloquent prose is marshaled for this reflection of
Clarissa's. The diction is again vaguely Shakespearian, or perhaps rather reminiscent of the Metaphysical poets of the gen-
eration after Shakespeare: the bones with wedding rings mixed

in the dust are akin to Donne's "bracelet of bright hair about the bone," and, in a more contemporary reference in the Metaphysical mode, the gold of the wedding rings is carried forward in the gold fillings "of innumerable decayed teeth," an image at once macabre and haunting. The vast temporal horizon opened up in the novel both backward and forward is, I would suggest, distinctly modernist. By and large, this is not the way nineteenth-century novelists thought of their world, though there are anticipations of such a perspective in Melville and in some of Dickens's metaphors, such as the lumbering presence of megalosaurus in the London fog at the beginning of *Bleak House*. The cultural life of the present city, in an age of archeological discovery and the imaginative assimilation of geological time, is seen as an evanescent moment against a daunting background of eons. A related habit of imagination leads Bely to end *Petersburg* with an image of the moldering Egyptian Sphinx and Joyce to line up his Dublin with the archaic worlds of the ancient Greeks and Hebrews.

The most spectacular instance of this dissolution of temporal boundaries under the aspect of eternity is the old beggar woman, singing unintelligibly in the street, "the voice of an ancient spring spouting from the earth," who is observed chiefly by Peter but by Rezia as well:

> Through all ages—when the pavement was grass, when it was swamp, through the age of tusk and mammoth, through the age of silent sunrise, the battered woman—for she wore a skirt—with her right hand exposed, her left clutching her side, stood singing of love—love which has lasted a million years, she sang, love which prevails, and millions of years ago, her lover, who had been dead these centuries, had walked, she crooned, with her in May; but in the course of ages, long as summer days, and flaming, she remembered, with nothing but red asters, he had gone; death's enormous sickle had swept those tremendous hills, and when at last she laid her hoary and immensely aged head on the earth, now become a mere cinder of ice, she im-

plored the Gods to lay by her side a bunch of purple heather, there on her high burial place which the last rays of the last sun caressed; for then the pageant of the universe would be over. (p. 81)

This weird and darkly enchanting meditation is presumably attributable to Peter, who has been listening to the old woman's song, but it seems to merge with the implicitly authorial view of the narrator who mediates the interior monologues of all the characters in the novel and thus puts more of a unitary imprint on everything than is the case in the play of different voices in Joyce's use of stream of consciousness. As a representation of the transience of civilizations and of the great cities in which they are concentrated, it combines the long backward and forward temporal projections that we have just noted. The old beggar woman, transformed into a mythic figure persisting through the ages, carries us back to the prehistoric era of the mammoths and forward to the extinction of life on earth (a more extreme point than the one in which future antiquarians will be finding wedding rings among crumbling bones)—the same Laplacean notion of sun-death that the late Dickens toys with in his metaphors, here powerfully focused in the image of "the earth, now become a mere cinder of ice," when "the pageant of the universe would be over." The passage plays ironically, caustically, yet somehow also respectfully with the worn idea of "love's eternal song." Love attaches us to life; the individual life lasts but a moment; and even the life of all earth's creatures is bound to come to an end; yet love remains a human defiance of inevitable extinction, it "prevails," its song goes on, though grotesquely garbled to the point of incoherence by the process of decay: "Still the old bubbling burbling song, soaking through the knotted roots of infinite ages, and skeletons and treasure, streamed away in rivulets over the pavement and all along the Marlyebone Road, and down towards Euston, fertilising, leaving a damp stain."

In this way the overflowing presentness of the city, its enrapturing variety and intensity as the collective manifestation of
life here and now, is played off against the vision of the city as
a poignant instance of the ephemerality of all things. Metaphor
enacts a key role in both perspectives. I would suggest that
whereas in Dickens metaphor serves to *realize* the subject in
often surprising, revelatory ways, in Woolf metaphor is chiefly
used to *interpret* the subject, to embody an attitude toward it or
evoke a mood it inspires in the observer. The metaphor here of
the song as a burbling spring (which in the next paragraph leads
to the wry representation of the old woman as a rusty pump)
conveys the notion of garbled sound together with the idea of
a fructifying life force, while also suggesting, quite unsentimen-
tally, that the stream, however it may soak "the knotted roots
of infinite ages," can effect no grand transformation in the face
of universal obliteration, and is destined to leave behind it in
the end only "a damp stain." Focused on the urban here and
now, metaphor as it is played with by different characters variously communicates the observer's sense of excitement over the
teeming life of the streets, the parks, the houses—the city as a
vast lap filled with angular odds and ends of people and buildings (Clarissa); a double-decker bus, with a view from the upper
level, as a frigate sailing through the waves of the city (her
daughter Elizabeth); London at eventide as a woman slipping
off her print dress and arraying herself in blue and pearls (Peter). All this makes for a certain aestheticization of the city, but
the perception of urban beauty is grounded not in any idea that
the city is necessarily a pretty sight but rather in an awareness
that it manifests the engaging multifariousness of modern life
itself.

The rendering of urban existence through the minds of the
fictional personages takes a rather unanticipated step beyond the
immediacy of sensory experience that Flaubert realized so brilliantly in *The Sentimental Education*. Because the consciousness
of these characters, in keeping with the sensibility of their au-

thor, is so athletically metaphorical (in sharp contrast to the consciousness of Flaubert's protagonist), what we see of the city is what the mind actively makes of it, or even how the mind transforms it. London, with a good deal of attention to its glamour and only brief notice of its grit and grimness, is an arena of exhilaration, the place where a modern social being can feel fully alive, as in pastoral young lovers are harmoniously alive on the greensward. What makes this vision of the city more than naive celebration is that it is asserted against the shadow of a darker view, in which the same narrated consciousness that exercises the freedom to transform the scene though metaphor is led to reflect on this so abundantly present city as an image of ineluctable transience. In this second perspective, the metaphors are not figures of gorgeous array and maritime adventure but death's sickle, cinders of ice, and the irrevocable end of splendid pageantry. These two complementary activities of the metaphorical imagination give us a modern metropolis palpable in its distinctive sights and sounds and motions that is at the same time a virtually allegorical figure of human existence both in its pulsing vitality and its ultimate destiny of decay. Although one might speak of a "representation" of the city—or at least of certain selected bits and pieces of it—in *Mrs. Dalloway*, what Woolf actually offers is a long series of poetic meditations, set in a minimal narrative frame, on the city as a theater of vitality and transience, the city as an image of the human condition.

7

Joyce

Metropolitan Shuttle

JOYCE'S *ULYSSES* OFFERS a
more variously ample imagining of the city than any other modern novel. The distinctive aspects of the representation of urban
experience that we have been following from Flaubert onward
are all present here in a stepped-up version, whirling around in
wild and often extravagant circulation. The imprint on the mind
of the flotsam and jetsam of the bustling city streets is inten-
sified in this novel, with the sense of disjunctive perception
heightened by the stream-of-consciousness technique, which is
arguably the ultimate fulfillment of Flaubert's narrative practice
of showing everything through the character's eyes. The stream
of consciousness also makes more prominent the interweaving of perception and memory evident in Woolf's interior monologues, for the movement of the mind, represented in its rapid
leapfrogging from sensory data to recollection, constantly follows paths here of free association and fantastic elaboration.
This means that the modern urban predisposition to phantasmagoria is generated by the mind itself rather than by the nature of the urban reality, as in Flaubert and Bely. Stephen, walking along Sandymount Strand and contemplating the waters of

Cock Lake, listening to "a fourworded wavespeech," seeing the buffeted seaweeds "hising up their petticoats" superimposed on an image of the moon as a naked woman, with drowned men and the song from *The Tempest* floating on the errant tides of his reflections, has effectively generated his own phantasmagoria, as Bloom will do again and again in the central sections of the novel.[1] The explicitly phantasmagoric dramatic form of the sprawling Nighttown episode is thus an extreme realization of the exuberant circus of mental events that has been going on all along in the stream of consciousness of the characters. It is, moreover, in the hallucinatory half-lights of this whorehouse setting that Joyce opens up the apocalyptic perspective we observed in Dickens and Bely. In this case, however, because Joyce is interested neither in the impact of the city on the natural environment nor in any political menace (Dublin 1904 seems a much more tranquil place than Petersburg 1905), apocalypse can be played out as pure farce. When Stephen's ashplant smashes the chandelier, "Time's livid final flame leaps and, in the following darkness, ruin of all space, shattered glass and toppling masonry" (p. 583). But he has, after all, only done some drunken damage to a ceiling, and the Gasjet responds, with appropriate anticlimactic bathos, "Pwfungg!" A few pages on, in a more extravagantly farcical fashion, we get a whole apocalyptic panorama replete with screeching whores, hooting foghorns, dying soldiers, flying witches, dragon's teeth, and the apparatus of the Black Mass (pp. 598–599). Behind all this there may be some serious brooding on the nature of European history, famously described twice in the novel as a "nightmare" from which we are trying to awake, but its manifest intention is to be a spectacular exhibition of the histrionic fun and games of the fantasizing imagination. Apocalypse has lost its sting in Joyce's great comic novel.

Much of the new sense of the city registered by all these novels is a consequence of a new order of urban magnitude, and it must be said that in this regard Dublin is not one of the great

European cities. Its population in 1904, the year in which *Ulysses* is set, was not quite 300,000, which makes it somewhat less than a twentieth the size of London at this time. It also did not extend over a very large area as did London: walking seems a practical way to get between many points in Dublin, as one sees repeatedly in the novel. Faceless crowds and urban anomie are also not much in evidence in the book. On the contrary, there is at least a vestigial feeling of villagelike community in this Irish urban space: almost everyone seems to know that poor Paddy Dignam has just died and that Mina Purefoy is about to give birth; one cannot walk very far along these streets without bumping into Simon Dedalus or one of his progeny; and the elaborate interlocking of recurrent motifs in the novel is matched by an interlocking of recurrent characters, with familiar faces showing up almost everywhere. There is, nevertheless, a sense of the city's buzz of constant activity that pervades the novel, and one can say that the historical Dublin of 1904 resembles London and Paris at least in respect to its rate of growth: from the beginning of the nineteenth century its population had increased by a factor of five; and the bustle of traffic and pedestrians, the barrage of advertising (Bloom's trade, of course), the ubiquity of print journalism, underpinned by telegraphic linkage with the larger world (news of a maritime disaster in New York is bruited about), the presence of sundry arrivals from abroad, make this Dublin feel, despite its relatively small size, like a big modern city.

Let me propose as a way into Joyce's rendering of the city the little section which begins the Aeolus episode. That episode, one may recall, takes place in the editorial offices of the *Freeman's Journal* and is organized as a series of brief units set under boldface rubrics that parody newspaper headlines. The rubric for the first unit, in the boldface capital letters Joyce uses throughout the episode to simulate headlines, is **IN THE HEART OF THE HIBERNIAN METROPOLIS**, which is precisely our subject.

BEFORE NELSON'S PILLAR TRAMS SLOWED, SHUNTED, CHANGED trolley, started for Blackrock, Kingstown and Dalkey, Clonskea, Rathgar and Terenure, Palmerston park and upper Rathmines, Sandymount Green, Rathmines, Ringsend and Sandymount Tower, Harold's Cross. The hoarse Dublin United Tramway Company's timekeeper bawled them off:

—Rathgar and Terenure!

—Come on, Sandymount Green!

Right and left parallel clanging ringing a doubledecker and a singledeck moved from their railheads, swerved to the down line, glided parallel.

—Start, Palmerston park! (p. 116)

What is all this doing in *Ulysses*? It is, to begin with, a moment of pure mimesis of urban life. Because nothing like stream of consciousness is deployed in this episode, there is no effect of the refraction of a particular consciousness. Unlike the doubledecker bus in *Mrs. Dalloway*, transmuted by metaphor into a frigate, the double-decker and single-decker trams are made present in a way that seems almost unmediated, noisily headed off without figurative qualification on their appointed routes to the south and southeast of the city as the tram company timekeeper bawls out the stops they will make. The closely sequenced verbs at the beginning of the passage—"SLOWED, SHUNTED, CHANGED trolley, started"—are characteristic of the energetic rhythm and the syntax that are often observable elsewhere in the novel, a feature to which we shall return. That trait, taken together with the verbal route map announced by the stentorian timekeeper, suggests that the trams catch Joyce's imagination as an image of the incessant motion of the city as well as of its interconnectedness. Although I have called attention to the prominent pedestrianism in the novel, Dublin is also a place in which vehicular transportation is needed to reach many destinations, and the tram serves that purpose for much of the populace.

Trams were introduced in many European cities during the

late nineteenth century as an eminently practical means for conveying large numbers of people efficiently across rapidly expanding urban space. The earliest trams were horse drawn, but by the beginning of the twentieth century they had been electrified, as they are in this passage. (The "trolley" that the trams change, of course, does not refer to the cars, as in American usage, but to the overhead electric cables linked by a wheel-and-pole apparatus to the tram to power it.) This constant clanging to-and-fro movement of trams is the perfect manifestation of the literally electric dynamism of the city, and at least in this instance partakes of the novelist's celebratory sense of urban life.

Elsewhere, when we are inside the perspective of the character, the tram can also prove to be an annoyance. When Bloom, ambulatory voyeur, gets a sighting of an elegant young woman in silk stockings and gloves, a "noisy pugnose" tram slews between him and this vision of feminine charms while she mounts the tram, which swiftly carries her out of view. The lovely precision with which Joyce renders visual perception—here impelled by desire—in the kinetic urban scene is something to be appreciated: "The tram passed. They drove off towards the Loop Line bridge, her rich gloved hand on the steel grip. Flicker, flicker: the laceflare of her hat in the sun: flicker, flick" (p. 74). We have had abundant occasions to observe the fragmentation of visual experience in urban novels from Flaubert onward, with the human figure often seen not as a coherent whole but through the traces it leaves in disjunct body parts. In this instance that mode of seeing is clearly grounded in the physical set-up: as the tram moves rapidly out of Bloom's perspective, he can make out no more than a hat and a gloved hand on the steel grip, and with the object of perception in motion and the sight line partially blocked, vision in the bright morning sunlight becomes stroboscopic—"Flicker, flicker: the laceflare of her hat in the sun"—and then the first two words are repeated with the last syllable strategically lopped off, like Bloom's vision, "flicker, flick." (Like Bely, Joyce is a stylist acutely sensitive to the musical quality of language who is also often beautifully meticulous in the rendering of visual experience.) This moment also reminds us that the constant intersection of people in urban space makes it a breeding ground of fleeting desire, as Flaubert keenly grasped. Touch is involved as well as sight, for bodies crowded in a public conveyance can be a sensual provocation. The scabrous Lenehan will recall to his cronies a ride in a jarvey with the Blooms after a midnight party when he sat next to Molly and was able, so he claims, to enjoy a good feel of her voluptuous curves (pp. 234–235). Sex and the city is hardly an invention of American cable television, and we shall return to Joyce's resourceful exploration of the phenomenon.

Bloom watching the elegant woman going off on the tram is a vivid instance of the power of the stream of consciousness to represent immediate sensory experience. But as we observed in the case of Virginia Woolf, this kind of narrative technique also facilitates movement along a reflective or associative axis that can carry us back in personal and also cultural time. In this regard, too, the tram as a ubiquitous agent of bustling urban life plays an exemplary role. Bloom, walking by Trinity College on his way to lunch, is led to a many-linked chain of thought on existential themes by the passing before him of trams in the busy street. His reflections are worth quoting at length because they so strikingly illustrate both the rhythm and the range of the mental experience of the city as Joyce represents it:

> His smile faded as he walked, a heavy cloud hiding the sun slowly, shadowing Trinity's surly front. Trams passed one another, ingoing, outgoing, clanging. Useless words. Things go on same; day after day: squads of police marching out, back: trams in, out. Those two loonies mooching about. Dignam carted off. Mina Purefoy swollen belly on a bed groaning to have a child tugged out of her. One born every second somewhere. One dying every second. Since I fed the birds five minutes. Three hundred kicked the bucket. Other three hundred

born, washing the blood off, all are washed in the blood of the lamb, bawling maaaaaa.

Cityful passing away, other cityful coming, passing away too: other coming on, passing on. Houses, lines of houses, streets, miles of pavements, piledup bricks, stones. Changing hands. This owner, that. Landlord never dies they say. Other steps into his shoes when he gets his notice to quit, they buy the place up with gold and still they have all the gold. Swindle in it somewhere. Piled up in cities, worn away age after age. Pyramids in sand. Built on bread and onions. Slaves. Chinese wall. Babylon. Big stones left. Round towers. Rest rubble, sprawling suburbs, jerrybuilt, Kerwan's mushroom houses, built of breeze. Shelter for the night.

No one is anything. (p. 164)

Joyce keenly understands that urban life has a distinctive rhythm, which he registers in the distinctive rhythmic movement of his prose, and that this rhythm defines the urbanite's relationship with the world. One detects in the prose an element of syncopation, encouraged by the ellipses used to create the effect of the stream of consciousness, in which definite articles or verbs are dropped, thus suppressing an expected syllable, aborting the underlying approximately iambic pattern of English speech, and forcing a held beat between stressed syllables in sequence: "thíngs go ón [—] sáme," "tráms ín [—] oút." In a 1921 article in *The New Republic*, "Plus de Jazz," Clive Bell actually attacked Joyce, Eliot, and his sister-in-law Virginia Woolf (rather gently in her case) for their use of syncopation, which he identified as a subversion of rhythmic and syntactic propriety, and which he attributed, with the most unabashed racist flourish, to the nefarious influence of jazz.[2] The highly musical Joyce in fact evinces little interest in jazz, but one may infer that syncopation attracted him in part because it caught the energetic stop-and-start rhythms of modern urban life.

The stopping and starting are manifestly linked with the

passage of trams. The tram was obviously an adaptation of the principle of the railroad to intraurban transportation. One feature that distinguishes railroad travel from earlier forms of transportation is that it takes place, as Wolfgang Schivelbusch reminds us, on rigidly fixed tracks, for the most part laid down in straight lines, especially in Europe. (In America, where the cost of land was usually not an issue, tracks more often curved around natural obstacles.) In the urban setting, the trams, because they come and go on a closely sequenced schedule every few minutes, passing each other in opposite directions, make one more conscious than would trains that they are constantly shuttling back and forth between fixed terminals. In this way they convey a very different sense of the traversal of space from that experienced by someone riding on the back of a quadruped or even within a stagecoach. There is a new focus on sheer repetitive motion, punctuated by industrially metallic noise, and an accompanying tendency to reduce the space rapidly traversed to an abstraction, or at any rate to minimize any minutely concrete apprehension of it. (This is roughly what Schivelbusch says about the railroad.) Thus the "ingoing, outgoing, clanging" of the trams leads Bloom to an Ecclesiastian meditation on futile cyclicality and the transience of all things. The shuttling trams make him think of "squads of police marching out," probably because he was reflecting a moment before on the Sinn Fein and revolutionary movements. Violent revolution in Bloom's instinctively pacifist view is but another expression of futility: the revolutionaries assemble, and the armed authorities march out to beat them back, much as the trams pass back and forth on their fixed iron routes. From politics he moves to the two loonies in the street, perhaps because they are also a potential object (in this case, an apolitical object) of police attention. Then the frame of reference of the shuttle becomes existential, as the novel's principal instances of death and birth are brought in, the lately departed Paddy Dignam and the parturient Mina Purefoy. The daunting panorama of incessant birth and death, about which

Bloom shows himself more adept at arithmetic than he is elsewhere at popular science, leads him to imagine the bloody new-
born, invoking the language of Christian salvation, "washed in
the blood of the lamb," language that is repeated in other contexts in the book, but he characteristically turns theology into
an image of the natural physical circumstances of human existence, the baby bawling as the midwife cleans off the blood.

In the second paragraph of this passage, the tramlike to-
and-fro movement is manifested in the life of the city and its
relation to history. (Though the style is altogether different,
these reflections have a thematic kinship with ones we looked
at in *Mrs. Dalloway*.) A modern city, as the statistics of sheer
population growth suggest, is a place in motion, in a constant
process of transformation: "Cityful passing away, other cityful
coming, passing away too." Buildings, whole neighborhoods go
up, come down, go up again (a process of which Dickens, as we
noted, was keenly aware). In the midst of it all, the ordinary
citizen, vividly exemplified by Bloom, feels a loss of agency in
these cycles of change: "they" somehow reap the profits, own
the properties, oversee the rapid construction of jerry-built
housing, like the historical real estate developer Michael Kerwan
of whom Bloom thinks. The restless transformations of the contemporary city, in the concluding moment of this resonant meditation, carry Bloom's thoughts back through historical time, to
the pyramids (as in Bely), the Great Wall of China and Babylon
(he probably has in mind its ziggurats), the monoliths ("Big
stones") of prehistoric Ireland and the round towers of the pre-
Norman Irish monasteries. The modern city in its very dynamism spectacularly enacts the endless cycle of passing away and
coming into being of history itself. About all this, Bloom is led
to conclude gloomily, his thought probably colored by his need
to refuel with lunch: "No one is anything," a stark restatement
of the biblical Preacher's notion that everything under the sun
is vanity of vanities, a chasing of the wind. "No one is anything"
could serve as the motto for many works of modern literature,

beginning with Flaubert, but Joyce is an affirmative modernist, and the thematic, or perhaps psychological, task of the novel is to move beyond this bleak conclusion to an embracing of life in the face of change, decay, and inevitable death. A few pages later, Bloom will do just that through memory in one of his radiant evocations of the first rapture of romance with Molly. Later, in the penultimate Ithaca episode, he will reach an acceptance of life against loss and humiliation from what amounts to a cosmic perspective. That moment of resolution in turn will become a prelude to the grand affirmation of eternal renewal in Molly's soliloquy at the end. Beyond the mechanical shuttle of the passing trams, there is another kind of repetition, which is the perennial reassertion of the impulse of life that both Bloom and Molly embrace.

One episode in *Ulysses*, the Wandering Rocks, is explicitly constructed to provide a panoramic view of the city. It happens to be the episode most tenuously based on the Odyssey, which may reflect the fact that Joyce felt impelled to give us at some point an encompassing picture of the urban scene, a narrative move for which Homer offered no convenient precedent. The episode consists of nineteen short sections and involves more than nineteen characters. Most of these are represented chiefly through dialogue, a few through stream of consciousness. The to-and-fro motion of the city is here matched by a to-and-fro movement of narrative point of view from character to character—from the Very Reverend John Conmee S.J. to Blazes Boylan to Stephen to Bloom and to a variety of minor characters (Miss Donne, Ned Lambert, Martin Cunningham, and so forth). The episode begins, interestingly, with a pocket watch, taken out for resetting by the Reverend Conmee at the exact time of five minutes to three. The obvious reason for introducing the timepiece at the very beginning is as one of the many orienting devices that are deployed throughout *Ulysses:* the narrative that begins at eight o'clock in the morning can be followed step by step moving forward in chronological sequence to its conclusion at the unspecified hour before dawn when Molly's soliloquy grandly rolls back and forth between moments of her life from adolescence onward and this day of June 1904. It should be noted, however that watches continue to pop up in the Wandering Rocks. When Blazes Boylan appears, he draws out a gold watch to check the time: he is sending flowers—by tram, he stipulates to the florist—to Molly, and he wants to be sure they will arrive before his eagerly anticipated assignation with her (p. 227). Lenehan, concerned about the afternoon race on which he is betting, asks M'Coy, "What's the time by your gold watch and chain?" Perhaps the timepiece in question is absent or not functioning, for M'Coy instead peers into a shop window where he can make out the time from the clock there as a little after three (p. 233). Stephen pauses for a moment at the premises of William Walsh, clockmaker, who, pointing to his handiwork, proudly says, "Very large and wonderful and keeps famous time" (p. 242). And just before the end of the episode, in the crowd of gawkers observing the viceregal carriage (a counterpart to the ministerial or royal limousine in *Mrs. Dalloway*), John Henry Menton grips his "fat gold hunter watch" (a watch with a protective hinged cover) but does not check it for the time (p. 253).

There is an obvious but limited parallel between this array of chronometric devices and the recurrent ringing out of the leaden hours by Big Ben in Woolf's novel. In both cases, the reminders of the mechanical measuring of time hold together all the disparate human figures, headed off on the city streets in different directions, literally and otherwise; whatever the riot of differences among them, they are all part of the same objective frame, marked by the fixed passage of time. In *Ulysses*, however, we see mainly pocket watches, which involve a private appropriation and transportation of objectively measured time. Historically, the watches carried about by members of Parliament and other privileged types in *Dombey and Son* in keeping with the new requirements of railway time have come to be more widely used at this early-twentieth-century moment. But a time-

piece that you take with you wherever you go is at once a way
of plugging yourself into the shared temporal grid and a reflection of the private meaning time has for each person. In the
second respect, it complements the centering of narrative in subjectivity of the stream of consciousness. For Father Conmee,
three o'clock means time for him to continue with the daily
round of his pastoral duties: he will take a tram to go where he
needs to go, and, after getting off, will amusingly encounter a
young couple emerging from the bushes where they have obviously been engaged in behavior not sanctioned by the church
or defined by a timetable. Blazes Boylan checks the time in his
eagerness for the moment of sexual consummation with the voluptuous Molly. Stephen is invited to contemplate the timepiece
as a splendid artifact. John Henry Menton caresses his fat gold
watch in the sensual pride of possession but shows no interest
in the time it shows.

In keeping with this variety of timepieces, the Wandering
Rocks defines the liveliness of the urban setting of the novel by
deploying a richly various moving picture of life in the streets:
draymen loading their carts, schoolboys, sandwich men, a dancing master, an ambulance, a one-legged sailor begging and a
blind stripling (both of whom will return later), and the young
couple rumpled from their tussle in the bushes. All of this, in
order to be seen in its intrinsic vividness, needs to be conveyed
for the most part by an external narrator, though there are also
some brief moments of interior monologue. At the approximate
midpoint of the episode, when Bloom, then Stephen, appear, we
are given passages of actual stream of consciousness, the mode
of narration predominantly used for both those central characters. The episode then returns to dialogue and external narration, in which it continues to the end. The counterpoint of external and internal views in this episode of urban panorama
mirrors the overall design of *Ulysses*, which makes abundant and
wonderfully imaginative use of stream of consciousness but also
plays off that dense interiority against more external per-

spectives manifested in a variety of styles and narrative techniques. (*Mrs. Dalloway*, by contrast, has a single style, with certain modulations, and no external perspectives, a mode of representation that yields less of a sense of the city's full material reality than one finds in Joyce.)

From the beginning of this story about the novel and the city with Flaubert, I have drawn attention to the different sense of experience in the modern city produced by the concentrated superabundance of sensory data. This is the key emphasis of Georg Simmel's pioneering essay on mental life and the city that was picked up by Walter Benjamin. Joyce exploits this superabundance, interweaving outer and inner, as a rich poetic resource and an occasion for taking us into the crowded psychological space of the principal characters. Noise in the streets, the clanging of trams, people hurrying by, the shop fronts, merchandise displayed in the shops and on the streets have their intrinsic dense concreteness as part of Dublin 1904 and at the same time trigger chains of dynamic associations in the characters. Leopold Bloom, stopping at a bookstall in the middle of this episode, picks up a novel by the French author of soft-core pornography Paul de Kock entitled *Sweets of Sin*. (An actual work by this title has not been unearthed, and it may well be an invention of Joyce's in the manner of Paul de Kock.)

> He read where his finger opened.
> —*All the dollarbills her husband gave her were spent in stores on wondrous gowns and costliest frillies. For him! For Raoul!*
> Yes. This. Here. Try.
> —*Her mouth glued on his in a luscious voluptuous kiss while his hands felt for the opulent curves inside her déshabillé.*
> Yes. Take this. The end.
> —*You are late, he spoke hoarsely, eyeing her with a suspicious glare. The beautiful woman threw off her sabletrimmed wrap, displaying her queenly shoulders and heaving embonpoint. An imperceptible smile played round her perfect lips as she turned to him calmly.*
> Mr. Bloom read again: *The beautiful woman.*

Warmth showered gently over him, cowing his flesh. Flesh yielded amid rumpled clothes. Whites of eyes swooning up. His nostrils arched themselves for prey. Melting breast ointments *(for him! For Raoul!)*. Armpits' oniony sweat. Fishgluey slime *(her heaving embonpoint!)*. Feel! Press! Crushed! Sulphur dung of lions!

Young! Young!

An elderly female, no longer young, left the building of the courts of chancery, having heard in the lord chancellor's court the case in lunacy of Potterton, in the admiralty division the summons, exparte motion, of the owners of the Lady Cairns versus the owners of the barque Mona, in the court of appeal reservation of judgment in the case of Harvey versus the Ocean Accident and Guarantee Corporation.

Phlegmy coughs shook the air of the bookshop, bulging out the dingy curtains. The shopman's uncombed grey head came out and his unshaven reddened face, coughing. He raked his throat rudely, spat phlegm on the floor. He put his boot on what he had spat, wiping his sole along it and bent, showing a raw-skinned crown, scantily haired.

Mr. Bloom beheld it.

Mastering his troubled breath, he said:

—I'll take this one.

The shopman lifted eyes bleared with old rheum.

—*Sweets of Sin*, he said, tapping on it. That's a good one. (pp. 236–237)

Joyce understood more knowingly than any other modern writer that a culture—and a city as the capital of a culture—is a vast palimpsest in which one language is written, or indeed scribbled, on top of another. To put this in the terms that M. M. Bakhtin has vigorously set forth, the city is a prime arena for the clash and interchange of languages, each reflecting the values of the social, professional, or ideological subgroup from which it derives. (Again, the contrast with Woolf, who essentially has a single language for her city, is notable.) Joyce's Dublin, like modern cities elsewhere, is a city papered over with texts. Just in this panoramic episode, we have: the advertisement on the sandwich boards, the crumpled throwaway announcing the coming of Elijah (text turned into garbage, as in Dickens), the breviary leafed through by Father Conmee, the fragments of Milton and Blake floating in Stephen's stream of consciousness, the specimen here of genteel erotic fiction, an actual quotation (collage is part of Joyce's technique) of the *Freeman's Journal* for June 16, 1904, regarding a lunacy case involving a certain Potterton, and much, much more. The passage we are considering, as I shall try to show, is a striking microcosm of the fictional world of *Ulysses*. Given the centrality of the representation of consciousness to that world, this means in part that it is an arresting instance of how circumambient reality activates the motions of the mind and of how the representation of the mind and of the reality outside it sets up an antiphonal play between the two.

The city is, among other things, a great emporium, displaying its multifarious wares to excite the desires, as happens here in a plainly erotic sense. Bloom, randomly opening *Sweets of Sin*, comes upon this description of a rousing sexual encounter, strung together (in a delicious parody) out of a series of clichés ("luscious voluptuous kisses," "opulent curves," "perfect lips") and fake-elegant French mannerisms ("déshabillé," "heaving embonpoint"). The banal phrase "the beautiful woman" mesmerizes Bloom because it obviously makes him think of Molly. Raoul thus becomes a corny fictional stand-in for Blazes Boylan, whose scheduled afternoon visit to 7 Eccles Street Bloom fears, and this equation will be repeated as the novel goes on. What makes the parody so piquant and amusing is the drastic textural contrast with the language of Bloom's stream of consciousness that immediately follows. The stream of consciousness in this instance provides us a rendering of the imaginative or fantasizing experience of reading. Conning the page, Bloom feels showered with warmth (this is still the narrator reporting about Bloom), then enters imaginatively into the sexual scene, identifying for the moment with Raoul, the sumptuous yielding female flesh beneath him. This sad figure of rather shaky virility becomes as he reads a fierce sexual predator, living up to his given name, Leopold, which is probably alluded to in the last word of the cries of sexual ecstasy: "Feel! Press! Crushed! Sulphur dung of lions!" Consciousness, because it is not obliged to conform to norms of literary or social decorum, can be an agent of strong realism, in regard both to details observed and to diction. Thus, "Armpits' oniony sweat. Fishgluey slime" is an imagining of the sexual act with its accompanying secretion of fluids that makes the queenly shoulders and heaving embonpoint look silly. (It was this aspect of Joyce that no doubt led to feelings of discomfort in Virginia Woolf, which are reflected in her famous remark about *Ulysses* that it was not necessary to break all the windows in order to get a breath of fresh air.)[3]

The brawl of competing languages is not limited to the contrast between the hifalutin', genteel-erotic hackneyed prose and the pungent physical concreteness of Bloom's stream of consciousness. After the climax of the sexual fantasy, Bloom abruptly deflates his own balloon as he often does elsewhere, with "Young! Young!" expressing his melancholy perception of himself, a man toward the end of his thirties, as someone now forever beyond the raptures of the idealized young lovers in the book. Then, in an amusing effect of montagelike transition, the narrator, leaving Bloom's consciousness, jumps to the "elderly female, no longer young," seen coming out of the court building. This whole paragraph is in legalese, a bit of it, as I have noted, actually a collage snippet from the day's newspaper. The mutually qualifying juxtaposition of different languages that Bakhtin calls heteroglossia is in lively play here, as throughout the novel. Beyond the stylized language of a particular literary genre (soft-core pornography) and the blunt immediacy of the language of consciousness, social institutions—here, the law— with their own specialized languages grind on in their rounds of daily activity that are also part of urban life. Following the excursion into the legal realm, the deliberately unpleasant paragraph devoted to the shopkeeper's spitting phlegm on the floor (still from the narrator's perspective) introduces a different literary dialect—the gritty, unflinchingly specifying language of fictional realism pioneered by French writers from Flaubert to Zola, and, until Joyce, adopted by English novelists only in somewhat dilute form. (There is a good deal of it in the opening episode of *Ulysses*.) Joyce's impulse to plunge his readers, with a certain shock effect, into bodily realities hitherto veiled by literary decorum is evident in the discomfiting consonance between the shopman's phlegm, the rheum in his eyes, and the fishgluey slime prominent in Bloom's imagining of the sexual act.

Although Bakhtin invites us to conceive this kind of interplay of languages as dialogue, that might be a somewhat utopian construction of a situation in which clash, dissonance, and disjunction are the salient features. Compositionally, at any rate, what is visible here, as in much of this novel, is an energetic cutting back and forth between swathes of disparate linguistic materials that are assembled in a complex, aesthetically satisfying narrative whole. Fragmentation and discontinuity have been central to the novelistic representation of urban experience since Flaubert, and we have seen multiple instances in which these qualities induce in both characters and readers a sense of disorientation or of unsettling loss of control. Virginia Woolf registers the fragmentation in her interior monologues but in effect transcends it by pulling the bits and pieces into exquisitely woven nets of poetic metaphor. Joyce, favoring the more jagged form of stream of consciousness, zestfully embraces the fragmentation instead of seeing it as a source of consternation. The fragments in his treatment of them become a new kind of poetry that affirms simultaneously the inventive energies of the mind and the concrete particularities of everyday experience. Let me offer a last, brief example, when Bloom is on his way to lunch in the Lestrygonians episode. It will bring us back to our point of departure, the movement of trams in the city:

> Gleaming silks, petticoats on slim brass rails, rays of flat silk stockings.
> Useless to go back. Had to be. Tell me all.
> High voices. Sunwarm silk. Jingling harnesses. All for a woman, home and houses, silk webs, silver, rich fruits, spicy from Jaffa. Agendath Netaim. Wealth of the world. (p. 168)

Bloom is remembering, I think, the young woman in the silk stockings who escaped his vision after mounting the tram. The staccato rhythm of the stream of consciousness produces visually a rapid sequence of flickering images, the female accoutrements glimpsed on the departing tram—"Gleaming silks, petticoats on slim brass rails, rays of flat silk stockings." Indeed, the shuttling movement of the trams is virtually an externalization of the movement of the mind shuttling between images and ideas. It is a mark of the richness of *Ulysses* that the ideas go back in cultural as well as personal time. "All for a woman" looks like an allusion to Helen of Troy (still another of Molly's avatars), who figures importantly in the other Homeric epic. The silk webs, silver, and spicy fruits tug us toward the sunlit world of the ancient Mediterranean, much on Bloom's mind. This provides the associative segue to the "Zionist" theme—Jaffa (where Bloom had imagined piles of oranges) and Agendath Netaim (actually, Joyce's scrambling of the Hebrew *Agudath Not'im*, Planters' Association). Beneath the seemingly disjunct surface of the stream of consciousness, as Joyce's commentators have abundantly shown, lies the elaborate artifice of architectonic design executed through recurrent motifs: Bloom, at once Ulysses and the Wandering Jew, longs to return from exile to the land flowing with milk and honey which is also Ithaca and faithful Penelope; and all of that is implicit in these lines. This is not a novel about desire fulfilled but about the healthiness of desire constantly reasserting itself, despite all frustrating experience, as a stubborn attachment to life. Walking through the busy streets of the city on this bright June day, Bloom bathes in a spate of images, sounds, and odors triggering memories recent and distant and a profusion of thoughts. His mind races back and forth among all of these, exulting in their multifarious abundance, accepting the desires they arouse as a reverential response to the beauty of life. For the moment, at any rate, this urban pedestrian and modern Ulysses feels blessed in all that rains down upon him in the street. From his thoughts on Jaffa and the wealth of the world, he goes on to: "Perfumes of embraces all him assailed. With hungered flesh obscurely, he mutely craved to adore."

As we have seen from the outset of our considerations, the modern city, in certain ways a qualitatively new organization— or in some respects disorganization—of collective life, has often been perceived by writers as a grave problem, a source of disorientation and alienation. But the power of these negative literary images of the city should not lead us to make excessive claims about modern urban life as something totally unprecedented or necessarily disastrous. The new European metropolises certainly reflect momentous and in some ways troubling change, but they also manifest continuities with the nature of urban life in previous eras. It is, I think, the aspect of continuity that underlies *Ulysses*, providing a warrant for its allusive meshing of modern Dublin with Homer's Ithaca and the Promised Land of the Bible. The concentration of habitations, crowds in the street, and cultural institutions in the city has always had its excitements, and what Joyce sees in expanding Dublin at the beginning of the twentieth century is no more than an intensification and variegation of such excitements, with the trams, the telegraph, the printing press accelerating the back-and-forth movement of people and information that has been manifested in cities through the ages. This is a perception akin to Virginia Woolf's in *Mrs. Dalloway*, though Joyce embraces the energies and especially the sheer heterogeneity of the city more zestfully that she does. His Dublin reflects the distinctive nature of a twentieth-century urban world but also is not unlike cities as they have been through the long course of history, going back to ancient Athens and Jerusalem—places where people are brought together in an expression of collective vitality that has the power to enhance the lively sense of experience of the individual urban person. The city thus becomes for Joyce the fittingly engaging theater for the grand affirmation of life that in the end his novel will express.

8

Kafka

Suspicion and the City

I<small>T MAY SEEM AT FIRST</small> an eccentric choice to conclude these considerations of the city and the language of the novel with Kafka. He, it might be objected, is by no means a realist, and so what possible bearing could his fiction have on representations of the modern European city? In fact, the focus of my analysis throughout has been not on an objective entity called the modern city which is somehow "reflected" in the novel but rather on a certain range of experience, much of it quite distinctive in nature, that is generated by the new metropolises and for which innovative writers found compelling means of expression. This is not to say that every novelist is a solipsist who simply makes up his or her own city but rather that every urban novel, even a solidly realist one, is an imaginative mediation of the experience of the city. The city itself through the nineteenth century and on into the age of modernism remains after all a describable historical entity with its demographic patterns, its utilization of new technologies, its architectural and geographical configurations, and with the ecological consequences of its industries and its concentration of population. As we have seen, the artistic antennae of some of our writers pick up what is disorienting or dismaying in the new cities, while others respond to the excitement of the highly charged urban world. If the major European cities of this period, typically doubling in population every few decades, rapidly throwing up tenements and large apartment buildings to house their masses, dissolve older feelings of community and heighten a sense of isolation in the individual, Kafka articulates the ultimate psychological and ontological effects of this condition in his one exclusively urban novel, *The Trial*. Begun in 1914 (and of course never entirely completed), at the very time Joyce was working on *Ulysses* and Bely on *Petersburg*, it appeared posthumously in 1925, two years after *Mrs. Dalloway* and three years after *Ulysses* and the final version of *Petersburg*.

Kafka's *attitude* toward the city, which may usefully serve as a preface to his novelistic representation of the experience of the city, is clearly delineated in a few of his brief parables. One of the texts in the early part of Genesis that he was drawn to several times is the story of the Tower of Babel. It clearly fascinated him in part because of the vexing issue of languages that repeatedly engaged him as a German writer in multilingual Prague but, even more, because it is a powerful expression of the antiurban bias that marks much of the Hebrew Bible. He responds to this bias strikingly in the most elaborate of his Babel parables, "The City Coat of Arms." In it, the building of the Tower, a kind of logical extension of the building of the city, is understood as an overreaching presumption of collective human effort, doomed to failure by humanity's inveterate divisiveness and by its deficiency of willed persistence in great efforts. Life in the city eventually becomes intolerable to its inhabitants, and thus the parable ends, oddly and instructively, with a hunger for apocalypse: "All the legends and songs that came to birth in that city are filled with longing for a prophesied day when the city would be destroyed by five successive blows from a gigantic fist."[1] The apocalyptic prospect that induces nervousness in

Dickens and deep anxiety in Bely is here eagerly embraced by the desperate denizens of Kafka's emblematic city.

Another brief piece which is symptomatic of Kafka's attitude toward the city is his reflection on that ubiquitous vehicle of urban transportation, "On the Tram." It will be evident what a different construction he puts on the tram from Joyce's. Here is the first of the three paragraphs of the piece:

> I stand on the end of the platform of the tram and am completely unsure of my footing in this world, in this town, in my family. Not even casually could I indicate any claims that I might rightly advance in any direction. I have not even any defense to offer for standing on this platform, holding on to this strap, letting myself be carried along by this tram, nor for the people who give way to the tram or walk quietly along or stand gazing into shopwindows. Nobody asks me to put up a defense, indeed, but that is irrelevant. (p. 388)

As with Leopold Bloom's observing the shuttling back and forth of the cars on their rails, the tram becomes the occasion for what amounts to an existential reflection, but with the crucial difference that it is viscerally experienced by this passenger on the tram. In this case, the tram moving from stop to stop on its fixed urban route brings home to the passenger his own loss of agency, "holding on to this strap, letting myself be carried along by this tram." Rolling along in a vehicle he himself cannot direct, he tells us, "I . . . am completely unsure of my footing in this world, in this town, in my family." What is more, he feels no connection with the crowd of people around him on the tram or outside it in the streets. On the contrary—and here our tram passenger edges close to Joseph K. of *The Trial*—he is vaguely apprehensive that these strangers in the urban crowd might accuse him of something, and he wonders about his right to be among them, even though "nobody asks me to put up a defense." The moving tram is not an embodiment of the to-and-fro energy or even of the cycles of existence of the city as in Joyce but of urban restlessness, instability, and the climate of suspicion in the faceless crowd. What follows in the next two paragraphs that conclude this brief piece is a narrative incident (or rather non-incident) bearing a certain kinship with Bloom's urban voyeurism, though again with an important difference. The speaker contemplates a young woman poised to get off at a stop and observes her dress, her face, her hair, and one ear. She is a source of wonder and, evidently, of erotic interest for the male passenger, but there is also a violation of boundaries in his contemplation of her that is in keeping with a certain abruptness or even violence in Kafka's general imagination of sexual encounter: "She is as distinct to me as if I had run my hands over her." Perhaps one begins to understand why the speaker, mingling amazed appreciative observation with fantasized sexual aggression, feels he might have to ward off some accusation from the people on the tram and in the street.

The city for Kafka is above all a place where one is alone, as his parable-like short narrative pieces remind us repeatedly. In a few of them, the aloneness is dramatized by the stance of the speaker at a window, looking out into the street. In *The Trial*, as we shall see, that situation is reversed, with Joseph K. conscious of someone across the way or up above him looking down on him from a window. The paradigmatic Kafkan urban setting is offered in a piece entitled "My Neighbor," perhaps with a tincture of irony, for what is at issue is contiguity in an office building and nothing like neighborliness. The narrator runs a small business of unspecified nature in which he oversees the work of two female clerks pounding away at their typewriters and filling in ledgers. A young man named Harras comes to rent the premises next to his. Harras repeatedly rushes by him on the stairs, barely allowing his face to be glimpsed, then bolts into his office and shuts the door behind him. "Like the tail of a rat, he has slipped through and I'm left standing again before the sign 'Harras Bureau.'" (Rodent imagery in general has a

certain disquieting attraction for Kafka, and we will later see
another instance of it.) The narrator fears that Harras is eaves-
dropping on his telephone conversations from the other side of
"the wretchedly thin walls." "Perhaps," the narrator worries at
the very conclusion of his uneasy report, "he doesn't wait even
for the end of the conversation, but gets up at the point where
the matter has become clear to him, flies through the town with
his usual haste, and before I have hung up the receiver, is already
at his goal working against me" (p. 425). Secretiveness, calculation, lack of human connection, relentless goal-driven,
business-motivated competition, suspicion of the other—we are
already in the world that has made *The Trial* for many readers
a somber model of modernity.

What is Kafka's relation to the repertory of distinctive technical resources for the representation of experience that we have
been referring to as the language of the novel? It is worth noting that he was an avid admirer of both the nineteenth-century
novelists whom we considered in detail, Dickens and Flaubert.
The connections between his own work and that of Dickens are
largely thematic. Arbitrary arrest, incarceration, stern judgment, and, above all, the systemic perversity of the law are preoccupations of both these writers, and there is an obvious link
in regard to the last between *Bleak House* and *The Trial*.[2] Beyond
such correspondences of theme, the cultivation of the grotesque
and, even more, the play of fantasy in Dickens's writing must
have surely appealed to Kafka, though both the fantastic and the
grotesque are given rather different expression in the fiction of
the Prague modernist. Flaubert, on the other hand, was a technical master for Kafka, as he was for many European writers of
the next two generations. He provided, to begin with, a model
of the writer as scrupulous artist, honing his work to perfection
through painstaking revision. (The imposing Flaubertian precedent of fiction as exacting artifice was probably one of several
reasons for Kafka's professed dissatisfaction with his own work
and for his inability to finish any of his novels.) But Flaubert

also brought to consummation in his novels a particular narrative technique, *le style indirect libre*, or narrated monologue, and
we had occasion to observe the virtuosity with which he deployed it in *The Sentimental Education*. Kafka evinces nothing
like Flaubert's interest in the rendering of the sumptuous fullness of sensory experience, but his more pared-down narration
in both *The Trial* and *The Castle* follows Flaubert's narrative
procedure in a fusion of the character's perspective or his un-
voiced speech with the mediation of the narrator. In Kafka the
ambiguity between the seeming authoritativeness of the narrator and the radical, chronically uncertain subjectivity of the
character is the aspect of this technique that is most pervasively
exploited. It was probably the moral and psychological richness
of just this ambiguity that led Kafka to abandon an initial experiment with using first-person narration for *The Castle* in fa-
vor of narrated monologue. The operation of the technique and
the force of the ambiguity are felt from the famous opening
sentence of *The Trial* onward: "Someone must have slandered
Joseph K., for one morning, without having done anything truly
wrong, he was arrested."[3] K., the modern urban isolate, a bachelor living alone in a roominghouse with no more than superficial contact with any of the people around him, is enclosed
from the start in a world of suppositions—the very mental activity that finds its perfect habitat in the narrated monologue.
Perhaps someone has in fact slandered Joseph K., for it is reported to us by the third-person narrator, but the suppositious
"must have" *(musste ... verleumdet haben)* has to be K.'s uneasy
guess, and the anxious defensiveness of "without having done
anything truly wrong" *(ohne dass er etwas Böses getan hätte)* is
surely attributable to K. as well.

The moment before the knock at the door by the oddly at-
tired emissary of the court, K. is seen in bed awaiting his break-
fast, which is usually brought in around eight but which on this
routine-upsetting morning has failed to arrive. In this supine
position, he is "watching from his pillow the old woman who

lived across the way, who was peering at him with a curiosity quite unusual for her." This is a preeminently urban moment. In a world of apartment dwellings crowded together in the packed space of the city, nominal neighbors who are in fact utter strangers peer at one another through facing windows. The physical setup is reminiscent of the one in Virginia Woolf where Mrs. Dalloway looks at the old lady in the window across the way and wonders about her hidden life, feeling stymied by the unbridgeable gap of "here . . . one room; there another." The obvious difference in this case is that K. watches the old woman—idly?—without showing any sign of curiosity about her (he is in fact singularly incurious about others except for their possible usefulness to him), while she looks back at him with what either is or at least seems to him to be unwonted, and not necessarily friendly, curiosity. We may infer that this curiosity has been roused by the appearance of a stranger whom she may have seen at the entrance of K.'s roominghouse, but given the limited subjective field of vision of the narration, that inference is no more than a guess, and perhaps the curiosity itself is merely the projection of K.'s anxiety, like so much of what he sees around him throughout the narrative.

A few minutes later in narrated time, after the arrival of the second "guard"—they are so designated from now on in the narrative because K. himself has concluded, "they must be guards" (p. 6)—he gets another glimpse of the woman in the window: "Across the way he saw the old woman, who had pulled an ancient man far older than herself to the window and had her arms wrapped around him" (p. 9). One can trace a line of quirky development in the novel from the significant detail in Balzac, in which particular elements of a given milieu are "organically" connected with each other and with the character, to the experienced detail in Flaubert, where what we get is the fullness of what the character sees and hears, regardless of meaning, to the aggressively gratuitous detail in Kafka. Indeed, I would argue against the countless interpreters of Kafka who

have sought to track down symbolic meanings that the distinctive imaginative life of his novels inheres especially in the vivid
gratuitous details, signifying nothing, like the "fitted black
jacket" worn by the first guard, "which, like a traveler's outfit,
was provided with a variety of pleats, pockets, buckles, buttons
and a belt" (p. 3), or like this old woman in the window embracing a still older male companion. They remain unnamed;
they cannot be said to have even a marginal role in the plot of
the novel; and only the most tortuous exegesis could make them
yield any symbolic meaning. And yet this fleeting glimpse by
K. of unknown neighbors sharpens his, and our, sense of his
sudden and acute predicament. Since the two old people are
standing at the window, we may assume, though we are not
explicitly told, that they are looking at K., that they confirm his
feeling of having become a spectacle. They also provide an unsettling contrast to him: he is young, just thirty, and very much
alone; the woman is old and the man she draws to herself is still
older, clasped to her in a gesture of solidarity, companionship,
or, for all anyone can tell, even senescent desire.

There is a peculiar narrative logic in Kafka through which
the gratuitous detail proliferates, thereby intensifying an effect
of arrestingly grotesque inscrutability. In the opening chapter
of the novel, K. is offered one last glimpse of the window where
he first saw the old woman: "Across the way, the old couple
were again at the opposite window, but their party had increased
in number, for towering behind them stood a man with his shirt
open at the chest, pinching and twisting his reddish goatee"
(pp. 12–13). In this beautifully efficient report, we learn that the
third person is much taller than the old couple, "towering behind
them," and that he is considerably younger, for his beard is still
reddish. The brilliance of imagining the gratuitous detail is especially manifest in the open shirt (a far less common mode of
dress in the early twentieth century than it is now) and in that
pinching and twisting of the goatee. In three rapid takes by K.
at the window across the way, the number of onlookers advances

from one to two to three. Perhaps we are even encouraged to infer the possibility of an infinite progression, the window-gazers staring at K. multiplying to myriads. The looming third person here could be a friend of the old couple, or their son, or—the possibilities are multiple—a party to some unseemly ménage à trois. In any case, the pinching and twisting of the goatee are testimony to some sort of tension or rapt attention or animality on the part of the third figure at the window. What-ever it may betoken, the gesture intimates a painful chasm of estrangement between K. and the unknown others who have their eyes on him. K.'s urban habitat, a labyrinth of office build-ings and apartment houses, many of them on the seedy side, in which people are closed off from one another in their pri-vate rooms, quickly turns into a breeding ground for paranoia. In this generalized and anonymous European city, projected out of the observed features of Kafka's Prague, we have come round 180 degrees from the flâneur of nineteenth-century Paris: the individual, instead of enjoying the pleasures of roaming spectatorship, has himself become a spectacle, the ob-ject of curious and perhaps contemptuous or hostile stares from windows.

The act of discriminating someone who is standing at a win-dow, perhaps looking down, returns in the penultimate moment of the novel, just before K. is stabbed through the heart. I do not mean to suggest that windows run through *The Trial* as a recurring motif, in the way motifs are deployed quite con-sciously by Joyce or by Dickens more intuitively. As far as one can make out from the incomplete state of the novels, Kafka does not seem to have wanted to use this sort of globally uni-fying device. What the window at the end amounts to is a kind of da capo gesture: K. at the beginning is aware of someone looking at him from a window, and at the end he thinks he sees someone else perhaps looking at him from another window, though both his seeing and the looking are shrouded in ambi-guity. The two executioners have briskly walked K. to an abandoned stone quarry outside of the city, but we never entirely leave the city in this novel, for alongside the quarry stands a building, clearly inhabited, "which was still quite urban" (p. 229). As one of the two men pulls out a double-edged butcher knife from inside his frock coat, K. looks upward:

> His gaze fell upon the top story of the building adjoining the quarry. Like a light flicking on, the casements of a window flew open, a human figure, faint and insubstantial at that distance and height, leaned far out abruptly, and stretched both arms out even farther. Who was it? A friend? A good person? Was it just one person? Was it everyone? Was there still help? Were there objections that had been forgotten? Of course, there were. Logic is no doubt unshakable, but it can't withstand a person who wants to live. (pp. 230–231)

In a novel relentlessly concerned with illusory perception, a phenomenon magnified by the isolation of the perceiver in urban space, this last sighting of a human figure at a window is a culminating mirage. The top-story window, unlike the window across the way with the old woman, is at a great distance from K., heightening the uncertainty. Perhaps he really sees a human figure there, though even that is not entirely sure. In contrast to the curious gaze of the old woman standing behind a closed window, this figure appears to be reaching out through an open window. But does he or she even see K. down below? Is this in any way a gesture of reaching out to him or rather a movement entirely unrelated to him, perhaps a simple act of immersion in the fresh air at the heights of the building? The language of K.'s narrated monologue here strongly suggests that the notions he entertains about the far-off figure are a fantasy of desperation. Indeed, when he thinks, "Was it just one person? Was it everyone?" *(Waren es alle?)*, he virtually admits that what he sees is projection, not perception. Like the initial figure in the window who increased from one to two to three, this tantalizing image up above may not be one but many, *alle*, now imagined by K. as a possible source of salvation rather than as a judgmental starer. The flip side of the emotionally distanced, suspicious or curious urban gaze is this desperate hunger, when it is already too late, for a gaze of compassion. But K., to the very end, is an extremely bad, if urgent, observer because he can never see anything except in the dubious light of its bearing on his case. Unlike his closely related counterpart in *The Castle*, he is himself a certified bureaucrat, and as a slave to the mind-set of bureaucracy—which is the administrative system par excellence of the metropolis—he can imagine his predicament only in terms of bureaucratic procedure: his underlying problem throughout the book is that he unquestioningly buys into the bureaucracy of the Law, however arbitrary or crazily capricious it may seem. And so now, when he looks up above for help, in one respect like the speaker in Psalms who says, "I will lift up mine eyes unto the hills, from whence cometh my help," his definition of help continues to be procedural: "Were there objections that had been forgotten?" If there is really a person at the window on high, he or she is transformed by the habit of mind behind K.'s gaze from an object of perception to a potential instrument in a system of bureaucratic manipulation. K. thus confirms his own aloneness, unto death.

Much of the voluminous interpretation of *The Trial* has been devoted, understandably, to the nature of the Law. In keeping with our focus on the novelistic rendering of the tenor of experience in the modern city, it may be helpful to consider how urban space is imagined in this novel. That, in turn, might throw some light on the Law as well.

The European Anycity in which all of the action occurs is a crowded, untidy place exhibiting a tendency to the accumulation of dirt and junk in entire neighborhoods as well as in the corners of the various chambers within. The neighborhood where Titorelli, the official painter to the court, lives, offers a revealing if perhaps extreme image of the atmosphere that pervades the novel:

The buildings were darker, the narrow streets filled with filth floating slowly about on the melting snow. In the building where the painter lived, only one wing of the great double door stood open; at the bottom of the other wing, however, near the wall, there was a gaping hole from which, just as K. approached, a disgusting, steaming yellow fluid poured forth, before which a rat fled into a nearby sewer. At the bottom of the steps a small child was lying face down on the ground crying, but it could hardly be heard above the noise coming from a sheet-metal shop beyond the entranceway. The door of the workshop stood open; three workers were standing around some object in a half-circle, beating on it with hammers. A great sheet of tin hanging on the wall cast a pale shimmer that flowed between two workers, illuminating their faces and work aprons. (p. 140)

Such descriptions in Kafka show a certain kinship with the representation of the sordid sectors of contemporary life pioneered by Zola, yet one senses that the purpose is different. This is surely not a "report" of the contemporary urban scene of the sort one would find in a Naturalist novel, and, indeed, the whole setting of *The Trial* is not exactly the contemporary scene but rather a bold extrapolation from it. The scurrying rat, the gush of excremental fluid into the open sewer, and the crying child are all plausible elements of a slum setting, and are precisely the sort of details that a different kind of novelist—say, Dickens—might use to rouse the reader's indignation over the degraded living conditions of the urban poor. For K., on the other hand, urban filth and disorder are the fitting scenic threshold to a meeting with someone connected with the Law, but connected in an essentially ambiguous way, like every single character in the novel from whom he seeks assistance or clarification. Immediately after seeing the rat and the sewage spout, K. will encounter a hunchbacked young girl who seems to have stepped right out of Svidrigailov's tortured dream near the end of *Crime*

and Punishment: "Neither her youth nor her deformity had pre-
vented her early corruption" (p. 141). The cluttered, filthy urban
milieu through which he moves, with these troubling glimpses
of deformity and corrupted innocence, are continuous with the
fragmentary revelations in the novel of the Law itself, a purportedly rationalized bureaucratic system devised to guarantee
the rule of just principle which in fact appears to thwart any
systematic coherence or actual justice, and which repeatedly
looks corrupt.

I am aware that I am beginning to edge these concrete images in a symbolic direction, the very kind of reading of Kafka
that I want to resist. The passage itself offers a welcome cor-
rective to any neat interpretation in the wonderful gratuitous
detail of the three workers beating with hammers on a metal
object of unspecified nature. What are they doing here? This is,
to begin with, a moment of sheer mimesis that Flaubert or Joyce
would have relished, with its vivid perception of the sheet of tin
on the wall casting a shimmering reflection that lights up two
of the workers. The presence of the sheet-metal shop is realistically plausible because this is a working-class neighborhood.
Work is going on here that is noisy, muscular, physical—the
very antithesis of K.'s paper pushing as a bank official and of
his flailing attempts to engage an elusive legal bureaucracy. K.'s
ultimate problem is of course in no way attributable to the fact
that he lives in a city, but the distracting noise and clutter and
the intractable disorderliness of the urban surroundings are an
external mirroring of the moral and spiritual disorder within
him. If life itself may often seem unmanageable in the sprawl
and bustle of the modern city, the city is the perfect setting for
this floundering everyman who has no enabling sense of purpose, whose inner world is an unacknowledged mess, and who
substitutes self-interested calculation for community and human
connection.

How does urban space make itself felt in *The Trial?* It is

sometimes crowded, which is hardly surprising, but it is especially instructive that K.'s first encounter with a court of the
Law is through a crowd:

> It turned out that there was indeed a narrow path free through
> the swirling crowd, one that possibly divided two parties; this
> possibility was further supported by the fact that K. saw
> scarcely a face turned toward him in the closest rows on his
> left and right, but merely the backs of people addressing their
> words and gestures solely to those in their own party. Most
> were dressed in black, in old, long, loosely hanging formal
> coats. This was the only thing K. found confusing; otherwise
> he would have taken it all for a local precinct meeting. (p. 42)

The confusion of realms as well as of perception is evident.
The premises of the Law give the appearance of housing some
sort of political meeting. It is uncertain whether the black-clad
figures are petitioners to the Law, spectators of the Law, or in
some bizarre way adjuncts to the Law's operation, though the
fact that they are dressed in loose black gowns in some way
confuses them with the justices whom Joseph K. is trying to
confront. We have observed the disorienting whirl of phantasmagoria in several other urban novels we have considered. What
Kafka in contrast gives us here and in many other scenes is the
hallucinatory clarity of a certain kind of dream: dreaming, you
find yourself in a strange place; everyone has his back turned
to you; almost everyone is wearing the same long black coat. It
is of course a cliché of criticism to speak of the dreamlike quality
of Kafka's fiction, but I want to swerve away from the sundry
routes of symbolic or psychoanalytic interpretation that these
dream-fictions have so often invited. What seems to me striking
about this scene, and, indeed, about most of the dreamlike passages in the novel, is the perfect continuity between the waking
world and the ostensibly oneiric one. The people in the loosely
hanging formal coats or gowns with their backs turned to K.
are an extension or a hyperlucid schematization of the experi-

ence of the individual in the urban crowd as Kafka typically imagines it. In the crowd, nobody sees you—the complementary opposite to sitting inside exposed to the curious gaze from the window across the way. In principle, the Law should be the administrative means of imposing order and direction on the unruly anonymous crowd. In K.'s first approach to a purported court of the Law, there is a disquieting confusion between the Law itself and the crowd, with its shapelessness, its anonymity, and its inherent divisiveness (here figured in what at least appears to the protagonist to be a split into two opposing parties). And K., desperately striving to establish his individual legitimacy as well as his innocence before the unspecified accusation of the Law, finds himself an ignored cipher in a literally faceless crowd.

Flaubert and Joyce scholars have actually drawn detailed maps of Paris and Dublin, plotting the movement of the action, respectively, of *The Sentimental Education* and of *Ulysses* over each of those cities, but the unnamed Central European city of *The Trial* is altogether unmappable. This is not only because it is a pure fictional construct assembled from bits and pieces of the Prague Kafka knew but also because space in this novel exhibits a propensity to contract alarmingly or, occasionally, to erupt. Alongside the familiar idea of an era of suspicion, one can see urban space in *The Trial* represented as a zone of suspicion. This is a process that is initiated at the very beginning with the old woman staring at Joseph K. It is manifested in the recurring images of claustral enclosure in which K. has a sense that he is somehow entrapped. Many exchanges take place in cramped corners. The Law is said to conduct its business in a network of attics throughout the city. Perhaps most pointedly, K. finds himself several times with insufficient air to breathe:

> "Couldn't we open the window?" K. asked. "No," said the painter. "It's just a pane of glass set in the wall; it can't be opened." K. now realized that he had been hoping the whole

time that either the painter or he would walk to the window
and throw it open. He was prepared to inhale even the fog with
an open mouth. The sense of being entirely cut off from the
outside air made him dizzy. (p. 155)

The rule of thumb seems to be that the closer one gets to
the Law, the less air there is to breathe. As if this stuffy atmosphere in the painter's studio were not bad enough, when Titorelli and K. leave the apartment and enter a long dank corridor
that appears to be a vestibule to a court of the Law, "air drifted
[from it] that made the air in the atelier seem refreshing by
comparison" (p. 164). The nearest approximation to a glimpse of
nature in the novel is the stone quarry at the end which is the
site of K.'s execution, yet even that, as we noted, has a tall
apartment building alongside it. Kafka shows a strategic awareness that the city cuts man off from nature, coating the earth
with pavement that is littered with the byproducts of human
activity, sequestering people in rooms within apartment dwellings with access through airless corridors and dark stairwells.
The protagonist of this novel is transparently not in touch with
himself, only with his constant anxiety over his interminable
case, but perhaps that fatal deficiency of self-knowledge is connected to the fact that he is also cut off from any sustaining link
with both community and the natural world.

The fantastic or oneiric aspects of *The Trial* do not feel gratuitous or arbitrary because throughout there is an integral connection between the tenor of K.'s inner life and the material
circumstances of the external world he inhabits, leaving the
reader repeatedly uncertain about which is cause and which is
effect. Despite a hygienic exercise of his sexuality in his weekly
visits to his mistress and in some more animalistic or calculating
expressions of it as the action unfolds, he remains an incorrigible
isolate, a man of mechanical routine and narrowly instrumental
rationality. The dreary neighborhoods and the cluttered chambers he enters in order to try to find some possibly useful

approach to the Law are plausible urban settings that also perfectly reflect his inner condition. That unsettling correspondence between outer and inner leads to certain moments in the
novel when what lies on the outside seems very much like a
projection or solid construction from what is going on inside K.,
perhaps below the level of his own conscious awareness. One of
the most riveting cases in point is the junk room off the corridor
leading from K.'s office at the bank. One evening, on his way
out after work, he hears groans from behind its door, which he
feels impelled to tear open violently. What he discovers is the
two guards who initially arrested him being beaten with a rod
by a man dressed in a tight-fitting, low-cut sleeveless leather
garment. They tell him that they are being punished because K.
lodged a complaint against them with the court. When K. opens
the door to the junk room again on the following evening, the
identical scene, as though it had been frozen in time till his
return, continues to play out from the moment when it broke
off. K., aghast, slams the door shut and hastens to instruct his
assistants, "Clear out that junk room once and for all. . . . We're
drowning in filth" (p. 87). This chamber of horrors just a few
steps from his bureaucrat's office strikes one as a scene projected
from the punitive aggression and the filth within K. himself:
there is a strong sense that, on some level, he has made it all
happen, that he is responsible for the guards and the flogger,
and not merely because he has lodged a complaint. But the city
as a whole in which he struggles to vindicate himself is drowning in filth—a real urban condition that for Flaubert meant the
violation of romantic aspiration, for Dickens an apocalyptic
threat to collective human existence, and for Kafka a deadly
failure of spiritual sanitation, an external image of his protagonist's incapacity to put his jumbled inner house in order.

The unfriendly, untidy city of *The Trial* is, in sum, a place
of constricting interiors, baffling streets, and narrow lanes,
where neighborhoods often seem telescoped into each other, and
where the bureaucratic orderliness of the office is contiguous

with a horrific junk room, as the pragmatic rationalism of the protagonist sits precariously over the junk room of his soul. Neighbors remain strangers, and for K. any familiar face is no more than a possible playing card in his life-and-death game with the Law. Just before the end, as the two executioners are hustling K. down a street near his roominghouse, he thinks he sees Fräulein Bürstner coming up a flight of stairs from a lane below, but here, too, uncertainty prevails. "He couldn't be absolutely sure it was her; there was certainly a strong resemblance. But it made no difference to K. whether it was Fräulein Bürstner; the futility of resistance was suddenly clear to him" (p. 227). It is, of course, bizarre that K. should in any way imagine Fräulein Bürstner might help him with his case; this can only be explained as his reflexive notion that somehow women— whether because he is able to engage them sexually or because he associates them with some vestigial idea of feminine compassion—will assist him in his defense. At this very late moment, however, K. no longer cares who the woman on the steps may be, for he has given up hope, and an identity that is of no use to him is of no concern to him.

Through all these considerations of urban experience in the novel, it is clear that what a writer will pick up in the city depends on his or her own sensibility, psychology, and preoccupations—on which urban frequency the writer is tuned in. I have not meant to suggest that there is an objective reality of the modern city which is rendered more authentically through the vehicle of the novel than it could be by other means (and the impressive achievements of painting, photography, cinema, and music as seismographs of urban experience, each medium doing the city differently, surely must be kept in mind). Rather, there are certain differing kinds of experience indigenous to the new metropolis which novelists, tapping their distinctive resources of figurative language and narrative techniques that take us inside the characters, can powerfully but also selectively convey to us, according to the varying predispositions of the different writers. The bustling city, as we saw in Woolf and Joyce, can be an occasion of celebration, though its alienating and ominous aspects have been acutely registered by novelists as far back as Dickens and Flaubert. Kafka surely evokes the dark side of the modern city as scarily as any writer has done. He is a novelist who has had abundant progeny but no really successful imitators. The spooky anonymous city of *The Trial* will have distant reverberations in the Bouville of Sartre's *La nausée*, in American hardboiled fiction, in the urban settings of some of the early novels of Alain Robbe-Grillet, in the fiction, more admired in France than in America, of Paul Auster, and in the work of many other writers. But Kafka, an absolute and highly peculiar original, pushes this particular vision as far as it will go. His fantastic city continues to feel urgently relevant to the real cities we inhabit almost a century later, as the imagined cities of the novel in general are refractions or even drastic transmutations of actual places that manage to give us back some of their essential qualities, illuminated by probing insight. It scarcely needs to be said that the modern city also breeds very different apprehensions of time, space, and human agency and relationship, but Kafka's sense of the labyrinthine city as a vast trap insidiously closing on the isolated errant self is a somber prospect that continues to haunt us in our own changing urban milieus.

Notes

Chapter 1. *Flaubert:* The Demise of the Spectator

1. Ann Banfield, *Unspeakable Sentences: Narrative Representation in the Language of Fiction* (Boston: Routledge and Kegan Paul, 1982).

2. Wolfgang Schivelbusch, *The Railway Journey: The Internalization of Time and Space in the Nineteenth Century* (Berkeley: University of California Press, 1986), pp. 47–48.

3. Margaret Cohen, *The Sentimental Education of the Novel* (Princeton: Princeton University Press, 1999).

4. Honoré de Balzac, *The Girl with the Golden Eyes,* tr. Carol Cosman (New York: Carol and Graf, 1998), pp. 22–23.

5. Priscilla Parkhurst Ferguson, *Paris as Revolution: Writing in the Nineteenth-Century City* (Berkeley: University of California Press, 1994).

6. Gustave Flaubert, *L'éducation sentimental* (Paris: Flammarion, 1985), p. 357. All translations from this novel are mine, and all subsequent citations are to this edition.

Chapter 2. *Flaubert:* Urban Poetics

1. Walter Benjamin, *Illuminations,* tr. Harry Zohn (New York: Schocken, 1968), p. 177.

2. Georg Simmel, "The Metropolis and Mental Life," in *The Sociology of Georg Simmel,* tr. and ed. Kurt Wolf (New York: Free Press, 1950), p. 410.

Chapter 3. *Dickens:* The Realism of Metaphor

1. Charles Dickens, *Our Mutual Friend,* ed. Michael Cotsell (Oxford: Oxford University Press, 1989), p. 221. All subsequent citations are to this edition.

2. Charles Dickens, *Bleak House*, ed. Stephen Gill (Oxford: Oxford University Press, 1996), p. 11.

3. Sergei Eisenstein, "Dickens, Griffith, and the Film Today," in *Film Form*, tr. Jay Layder (New York: Harcourt, Brace and World, 1940), p. 217.

4. Efraim Sicher, *Rereading the City, Rereading Dickens* (New York: AMS Press, 2003), p. 40.

Chapter 4. *Dickens:* Intimations of Apocalypse

1. Charles Dickens, *Dombey and Son* (London: Penguin, 1970), p. 290.

2. Charles Dickens, *Bleak House*, ed. Stephen Gill (Oxford: Oxford University Press, 1996), p. 11. All subsequent citations are to this edition.

3. Charles Dickens, *Our Mutual Friend*, ed. Michael Cotsell (Oxford: Oxford University Press, 1989), p. 267. All subsequent citations are to this edition.

4. In the discussion of this passage as well as of the next one, I have borrowed a number of sentences from my essay "Reading Style in Dickens," *Philosophy and Literature* 20, no. 1 (April 1996), pp. 130–137.

5. Michael Cotsell, *The Companion to "Our Mutual Friend"* (London: Allen and Unwin, 1986), p. 193.

Chapter 5. *Bely:* Phantasmatic City

1. A useful account of the idea of Petersburg in Russian culture can be found in Michael Holquist's "St. Petersburg: From Utopian City to Gnostic Universe," *Virginia Quarterly Review*, 48, no. 4 (Autumn 1972), pp. 539–557.

2. Andrei Bely, *Petersburg*, tr., annotated, and introduced by Robert A. Maguire and John E. Malmstead (Bloomington: Indiana University Press, 1978). All subsequent citations are to this edition.

3. I am indebted to my colleague Eric Naiman for calling my attention to this idea.

Chapter 6. *Woolf:* Urban Pastoral

1. Alfred Appel Jr., *The Art of Celebration* (New York: Knopf, 1992).

2. Virginia Woolf, *Mrs. Dalloway* (New York: Harcourt Brace Jovanovich, 1981), p. 71. All subsequent citations are to this edition.

Chapter 7. *Joyce:* Metropolitan Shuttle

1. James Joyce, *Ulysses* (New York: Random House, 1961). All subsequent citations are to this edition.

2. Clive Bell, "Plus de Jazz," reprinted in *Since Cézanne* (London: Chatto and Windus, 1922), pp. 217–230.

3. Virginia Woolf, *The Essays of Virginia Woolf,* vol. 4 (London: Hogarth, 1988), p. 434.

Chapter 8. *Kafka:* Suspicion and the City

1. Franz Kafka, *The Complete Stories,* ed. by Nahum N. Glatzer (New York: Schocken, 1971), p. 434. All subsequent citations of Kafka's stories are to this edition.

2. Mark Spilka has devoted a book to tracing these connections. See Spilka, *Dickens and Kafka: A Mutual Interpretation* (Gloucester, Mass.: P. Smith, 1969).

3. Franz Kafka, *The Trial,* tr. with a preface by Breon Mitchell (New York: Schocken, 1998), p. 3. All subsequent citations are to this edition.

Index